# REEDS

### 3rd edition

# MARITIME
## meteorology

**Maurice M Cornish**
Extra Master, FNI

and

**Elaine E Ives**
BSc

**ADLARD COLES NAUTICAL · LONDON**

D1380378

Published by Adlard Coles Nautical
an imprint of Bloomsbury Publishing Plc
50 Bedford Square, London WC1B 3DP
www.adlardcoles.com

Bloomsbury is a trademark of Bloomsbury Publishing Plc

First edition published by Thomas Reed Publications
Second edition 1997
Third edition published by Adlard Coles Nautical 2006
Revised 2009
Reprinted 2010, 2011, 2012, 2013, 2014

ISBN 978-1-4081-1206-9

A CIP catalogue record for this book is available from the British
Library.

This book is produced using paper that is made from wood grown
in managed, sustainable forests. It is natural, renewable and
recyclable. The logging and manufacturing processes confirm to
the environmental regulations of the country of origin.

Photo for chapter titles by Margaret Brain
Typeset in Bliss-Light 10/11pt

Printed and bound in Great Britain by
CPI Group (UK) Ltd, Croydon CR0 4YY

**Note:** While all reasonable care has been taken in the preparation
of this publication, the publisher takes no responsibility for the use
of the methods or products described in the book.

# CONTENTS

# PREFACE

In keeping with the original aim, this edition has been written primarily for serving and trainee deck officers on merchant ships and for fishermen. It is hoped that it will also be of value to yachtsmen and women and to all who have an interest in the sea and meteorology.

We have avoided what appeared to us unnecessary in-depth theory, but at the same time have given as complete an explanation of various points as we considered appropriate. The book is principally designed as a suitable textbook for those studying for certificates of competency. As far as possible it anticipates changes in examination structures leading to Maritime and Coastguard Agency (MCA) qualifications in the UK, and since similar changes are also taking place internationally, it should also appeal to other English-speaking readers.

We have taken into account the vast range of information available through the Internet and included website addresses which we considered most appropriate for further reading at the end of some chapters. The choice of websites was difficult as there are many hundreds.

A helpful Glossary is included and questions at the end of each chapter are designed to help the student to test his or her knowledge and understanding.

**Note:** We have used the hectopascal (hPa) as the unit of pressure, both in the text and marked on diagrams showing isobars. It has exactly the same numerical value as a millibar but is the preferred equivalent SI unit. Until now the millibar has been used in the majority of meteorological publications and is still used in weather forecasts for the general public. However, hectopascals are used by the World Meteorological Organisation (WMO) and are being steadily introduced and used in the same manner that Celsius has now almost totally replaced Fahrenheit as the unit of temperature measurement.

# ACKNOWLEDGEMENTS

The authors would like to thank the staff at the National Meteorological Library in Exeter, in particular Graham Bartlett and Steve Jebson, who both gave us generous assistance in selecting fresh illustrations of the sea state relating to the Beaufort scale and examples of clouds. Also our former colleague, Jef Forshaw, who was of considerable assistance when selecting alternative photographs. Finally, thanks to the individual photographers of both cloud types and sea state who responded willingly to our requests.

# ABOUT THE AUTHORS

**Maurice Cornish** served at sea as a navigating officer, principally in tankers. After obtaining his Extra Masters Certificate he commenced teaching in London before moving to Plymouth College of Further Education where he taught for 19 years. In 1982 he was appointed as Head of the Maritime Studies Department in Glasgow College of Nautical Studies. He retired from that post in 1992 and for some time acted as a tutor in meteorology by distance learning.

**Elaine Ives** graduated with a degree in physics from the University of Edinburgh in 1971. Since taking up a post as a lecturer at Glasgow College of Nautical Studies in 1978, she has lectured in meteorology and marine environmental studies. She is currently the Head of the School of Transport Studies, within the Faculty of Maritime Studies in the same college.

# 1 THE ATMOSPHERE

## Introduction

The Earth with its atmosphere, making their daily revolution together, could be likened to an enormous grapefruit having a skin which is thinner than rice paper. The difference in this analogy is that the 'skin' around the Earth is an invisible gas termed the atmosphere and held to the Earth by gravitational force. Its upper boundary has not yet been positively defined. In meteorology we are concerned almost entirely, with the lower region of the atmosphere called the troposphere, which extends from the surface to a maximum height of about 10 miles (compared with the Earth's diameter of about 6,900 miles). Because of its gaseous state, internal motions and physical effects it is mainly responsible for all our 'weather' (state of sky, clouds, precipitation, fog, mist and other meteorological phenomena).

### The composition of the atmosphere

Dry air is composed of a mixture of gases; within about 10 miles of the Earth's surface, which is the zone in which we are interested, the principal ones are nitrogen (about 78 per cent) and oxygen (about 21 per cent); there are also small quantities of other gases such as argon, carbon dioxide, helium and ozone. Finally there is a variable amount of water vapour in the atmosphere (see below).

### The importance of water vapour

The above gases are all, except carbon dioxide, more or less constant in proportional composition and are essential to life, but meteorological interest is centred chiefly on the amount of moisture (*water vapour*) in the atmosphere. The amount of water vapour present at any time is very varied because of changes in temperature and in the amount of evaporation from water surfaces and in condensation and precipitation. The changing quantities of dust and salt particles in the atmosphere are also of great meteorological importance.

## Vertical section of the atmosphere

Figure 1.1 is a schematic diagram showing a vertical section of the lower part of our atmosphere which is termed the *troposphere* and, from our earthbound viewpoint, is really the 'effective atmosphere'. This lower region is characterised by a fall in air temperature with height averaging about 0.6°C per 100 metres (1°F per 300 feet), a very appreciable quantity of water vapour, vertical currents of air, turbulent eddies and hence formation of cloud, precipitation and various atmospheric disturbances. Then comes a transition layer called the *tropopause*, immediately above which we find the *stratosphere* in which temperature change with height is small and a layer of *ozone* is found which protects the Earth from harmful effects of ultraviolet radiation. Above this comes the *ionosphere* which plays such an important part in the world of radio transmission and reception.

### Pressure of the atmosphere

Our atmosphere comes under the gravitational force of the Earth and although all gases are light they do have weight; the nearer to the Earth the greater the amount of atmosphere pressing down and the greater the weight or atmospheric pressure per square unit area of Earth's surface. At sea level the average atmospheric pressure is about 1,013.2 hPa; at a height of 3,000 metres this will have fallen to about 670 hPa. **It should be borne in mind that atmospheric pressure at any point is a force which acts horizontally in all directions as well as upwards and downwards.**

## Heating of the troposphere

The atmosphere is transparent to the short-wave radiation from the sun and receives little or no appreciable heat from this source. The Earth, however, is heated by the sun's rays and the surface air layer is warmed by contact with the Earth. This warmth is spread upwards by convection, turbulence and conduction. The latter process is, by itself, very slow. Thus air temperature in lower levels tends to be determined by that of the underlying surface.

## Variation of temperature with height

*(See Lapse rate in the Glossary.)*
Under normal conditions atmospheric temperature decreases with height from the surface up to the tropopause because the heating element (the Earth) has maximum effect at close quarters. Above the tropopause air temperature is no longer governed by upward air currents which transfer heat from surface levels. The reasons for this will become apparent in later chapters. The average lapse rate of temperature within the troposphere is about 0.6°C per 100 metres (1°F per 300 feet). The actual lapse rate varies appreciably from day to day and from

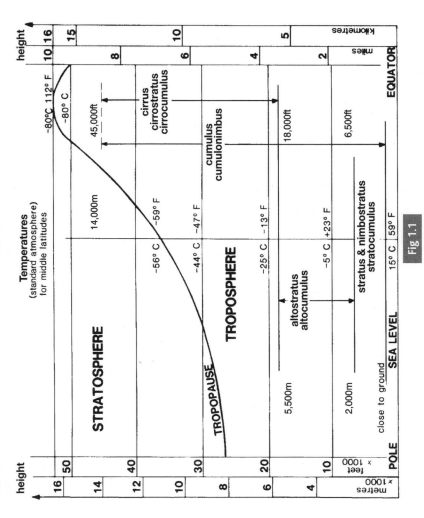

Fig 1.1

Note: Height equivalents are approximate

place to place, especially in levels near the surface, where considerable changes often occur within a few hours.

## Environmental lapse rate (ELR) within the troposphere

Figures 5.2 (a) to (d) show four characteristic graphs of Air temperature v Height within the troposphere. The actual values for temperature and height have been omitted on purpose. The SHAPE of the curve is one of the most important factors in the development of clouds, rain, hail, thunder and weather systems.

The diurnal variation of lapse rate in the lower levels of the troposphere is often very marked over a land surface, especially in fine dry weather with clear skies. In the mornings when the Earth is cool, a little before sunrise, the lapse rate is small and inversions (ie *increase* of temperature with height, see Figure 5.2 (b)) are common. After sunrise the land warms rapidly causing an increase in the temperature lapse rate, and this may become *steep* (ie large) by mid or late afternoon. As darkness approaches, the Earth cools once more and its temperature continues to fall throughout the night, thereafter the cycle is repeated. These effects may be modified or masked at times by the direction and force of wind.

## Variation of pressure with height

Atmospheric pressure at any level is the weight of the air above that level. It follows therefore that the pressure must always decrease with height. In the lower levels the average rate at which pressure falls is approximately 1 hPa per 27.7 metres of height, but the *actual* rate at any given time is governed by temperature.

In Figure 1.2, A & B are two columns of air having the same cross-sectional area and *the same mean sea level pressure*, but they have different mean temperatures.

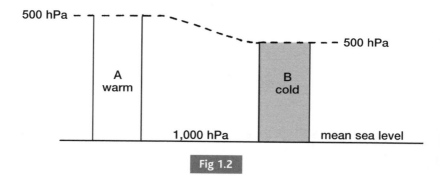

Fig 1.2

The cold air at B is denser and heavier per unit volume than the warm air at A, but the pressure *difference* between the top and bottom of each column is the same. Thus column A exerts exactly the same force as column B and the rate at which pressure falls with height must be greater in the cold column.

*Throughout this book the authors have adopted the use of hPa, hectopascals, which is the SI preferred unit rather than mb, millibars. Although the latter is still commonly used by the media it has been thought to be sufficiently important to use the preferred unit, Fortunately, they are the same numerically.*

# 2 SOLAR RADIATION AND TEMPERATURE

Radiation is a form of heat transfer which is completely independent of the medium through which it travels. All bodies, whatever their temperature, emit heat energy in the form of short electromagnetic waves which travel through space at the speed of light. The actual wave length depends on the temperature of the radiating body. The hotter the body the shorter the wave length and the more intense is the emission. At very high temperatures a body emits both heat and light, eg a fire. The surface temperature of the sun is something in the nature of 6,000°C.

Of the sun's radiant energy which strikes the Earth much is absorbed, thereby increasing the temperature of the surface which emits long invisible heat waves back into space. Some of the incoming short-wave radiation from the sun is lost through absorption, reflection and scattering by cloud. A thick cloud will reflect nearly 80 per cent of the radiation which it receives. Absorption is very little, probably about seven per cent.

Water vapour and cloud, when present, strongly absorb most of the outgoing long-wave radiation, some of which is re-radiated into space and some re-radiated downwards to the Earth's surface, and thus compensating in some measure for loss of heat by outgoing radiation. This is called the *greenhouse effect*. It explains why, when there is a thick cloud layer at night, the fall in surface temperature during the hours of darkness is less than on nights when there is a clear sky allowing *free* terrestrial radiation.

## Diurnal range of surface temperature

Soon after sunrise the incoming short-wave energy begins to exceed the *outgoing* long-wave emission. The temperature of the surface then starts to increase and generally reaches its maximum by about 1400 hours Local Time, after which it gradually begins to cool. All incoming radiation ceases when darkness falls and the surface continues cooling through the night until sunrise when the whole cycle is repeated.

Bodies which are good absorbers of heat are also good radiators and the converse is true. In general, land may be described as a strong absorber by comparison with a water surface which is relatively very weak. Thus the diurnal range in temperature of a land surface is much greater than that of the sea surface which, in ocean areas, is generally less than 0.5°C (the interior of continents may vary by 16°C (30°F) or more). The general pattern of diurnal variation in land temperature is often modified locally by weather. For instance, a change in wind direction might bring a much colder or warmer airstream into the region.

## Factors affecting the heating effect of solar radiation

### The inclination of the solar beam to the Earth's surface

This depends on:

* ❖ The latitude of the place.
* ❖ The sun's declination, which varies with the seasons.
* ❖ The daily change in the sun's altitude.

In Figure 2.1, the arc ER represents a portion of the Earth's surface. X and Y are two solar beams of equal intensity and having the same cross-sectional area. Beam X is directed at an oblique angle to the Earth's surface and its energy is spread over a relatively large area AB. Beam Y is nearly vertical to the surface and its radiation is concentrated onto the relatively small area CD. The pecked arc FGH represents the upper limit of the atmosphere, from which it can be seen that the beam X has to pass through a greater thickness of atmosphere than beam Y before reaching the Earth, and so will suffer a greater loss of energy due to reflection and scattering. Thus, all other things being equal, the heating effect will be greatest at area CD.

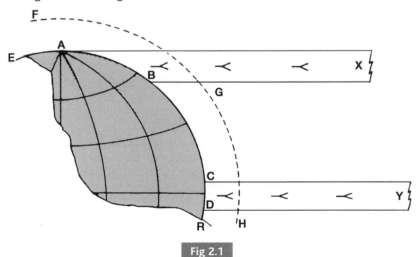

Fig 2.1

### The nature of the surface

Snow and ice surfaces **reflect** about 80 per cent of the radiation received. Dry soil, bare rock and sand, though poor conductors of heat, are very good absorbers and the heat energy received penetrates only a very shallow layer of surface amounting to a few inches. Hence there is a relatively high rise in temperature for a given amount of radiation. By contrast the temperature of the sea surface changes only a very little for the same amount of heat energy. The reasons for this are:

❖ The specific heat capacity* of water is much greater than that of land.
❖ The solar rays penetrate the sea surface to a depth of several metres.
❖ The stirring effect of the wind brings up colder water from below.
❖ Much of the heat received by the sea surface becomes rapidly used up in the process of evaporation.
❖ A water surface reflects solar radiation, especially at large angles of incidence.

**Air temperature** near the surface tends to follow that of the surface below. Thus the annual range, like the diurnal range, is greater over the interior of large continents than over the oceans. The main factors governing air temperatures at sea are:

❖ Latitude. Generally warmest within the tropics and subtropics.
❖ Season.
❖ Proximity to large land masses.
❖ Prevailing winds.
❖ Ocean currents.
❖ Upwelling of cooler water from the depths.
❖ The presence of ice or snow covering.

* The specific heat capacity of a substance is the number of joules required to raise the temperature of 1kg of that substance by 1°C. The specific heat of water is higher than that of any other common substance. Hence the gain or loss of a given quantity of heat brings about a smaller change in temperature of sea than of land.

# 3 HUMIDITY AND CONDENSATION

## Water vapour

This is water in the vapour state and although quite invisible, is always present in the atmosphere. The amount varies in both time and place. It is supplied by evaporation from the sea surface and, to much lesser degree, from lakes, rivers, snow, ice and other moist surfaces on land.

## Cloud and fog

These should not be confused with water vapour, cloud and fog are visible water droplets in the liquid state.

## Saturated air

The maximum quantity of water vapour which can be contained in a given volume of air is limited by temperature. The higher the temperature the greater the quantity of water vapour the air can hold. When the maximum possible amount is present the air is said to be saturated. Air which contains less water vapour than the maximum possible amount is said to be unsaturated. (Air which is unsaturated is often called *dry air* although it contains some water vapour.) If unsaturated air is cooled sufficiently it will become saturated. Further cooling will result in the **excess** water vapour being condensed into the liquid or solid state (visible water droplets or ice crystals).

## Dew point

The temperature to which unsaturated air must be cooled to become saturated is the dew point.

So long as air remains unsaturated and the amount of water vapour remains constant, the dew point will also remain constant although the air temperature changes. If air is saturated its temperature is its dew point.

## Absolute humidity

The water vapour content of the air at any one time and place expressed in mass per unit volume is absolute humidity – usually in grammes per cubic metre $(gm/m^3)$.

### Relative humidity

This is the ratio of the amount of water vapour actually present to the maximum amount possible *at the same temperature*. It is expressed as a percentage.

$$RH = \left( \frac{\text{Absolute humidity} \times 100}{\text{Saturation value at same temp}} \right) \%$$

Refer now to Figure 3.1 which is a graph showing the approximate saturation values of absolute humidity against air temperature. Exact values are of little or no concern to the mariner but the *shape* of the curve is of immense importance and this will become apparent in later chapters. The following should be noted:

**1** At a temperature of, say, 20°C the maximum possible amount of water vapour which the air can contain is about 20 g/m$^3$, whereas at 40°C it can hold about 50 g/m$^3$. Thus, the higher the air temperature the greater the saturation value of absolute humidity.

**2** Suppose a sample of air at a temperature of 40°C contains 20 g/m$^3$ of water vapour.

(a) Relative humidity $= \dfrac{20}{50} = 40\%$

(b) If the air is cooled sufficiently it will become saturated at about 20°C. The dew point is then 20°C. The dew point is constant through any changes of temperature above 20°C.

(c) Should the temperature fall below the original dew point (20°C) to, say, 10°C, then the new dew point would be 10°C, the absolute humidity 11 g/m$^3$ and a total of $(20 - 11) = 9$ g/m$^3$ of water vapour would have been condensed into visible droplets (eg fog, mist, cloud or dew). During such cooling below 20°C, the dew point will, at all stages, be equal to the existing air temperature.

**3** The curve shows that a fall in temperature of saturated air results in the condensation of the excess water vapour. The higher the initial dew point the greater the amount of water vapour condensed.

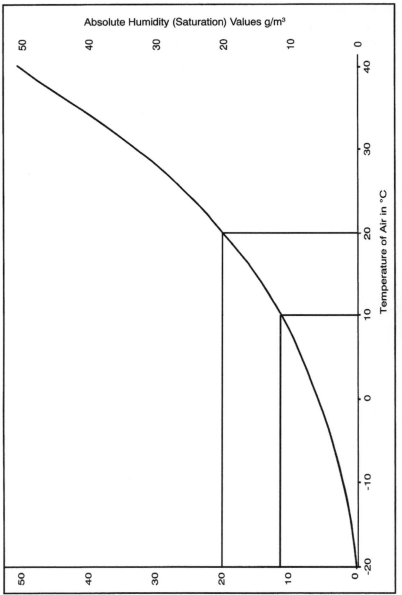

Fig 3.1

## Hygroscopic nuclei

Within the troposphere there is always present a varying quantity of very minute solid particles, such as dust*, salt from sea spray, soot and smoke from domestic and factory fires, plus other sources of pollution. Most of these particles are *hygroscopic* — that is, they tend to attract and absorb moisture. They are the nuclei onto which water vapour condenses, forming visible water droplets (cloud or fog). Without their presence any condensation would be highly improbable. They are most abundant in the levels near the surface, from whence they are carried upwards to higher levels by convection. In those industrial areas where there is a very high degree of smoke pollution, fog can sometimes form in falling temperatures a little *before* the dew point has been reached.

*Dust is not generally considered to be hygroscopic.*

## QUESTIONS

*Remember to use the Glossary*

### TEST QUESTIONS Chapters 1 to 3 (inc)

1 Describe briefly the characteristics and extent of the tropopause.

2 What is the average lapse rate of temperature within the troposphere?

3 In spite of the relatively high surface temperatures within the tropics, the temperature at the tropopause over the equator is much lower than over the polar caps. Explain why this is so.

4 Name and describe the processes whereby heat is transferred from the Earth's surface to the troposphere.

5 Write brief notes on the diurnal variation of temperature lapse rate in the lower levels of the troposphere.

6 Explain why atmospheric pressure decreases with height above sea level.

7 (a) What is the approximate average rate of fall of atmospheric pressure within the lower levels?
  (b) On what does the actual rate depend? Explain why.

**Solar radiation and temperature**

8 Describe the greenhouse effect on the Earth's atmosphere.

9 Define specific heat.

10 (a) Describe briefly each of the main factors on which the maximum temperature attained by a land surface depends for a given amount of solar radiation.
  (b) Account fully for the relatively very small daily changes in the temperature of the sea surface.

# 4 CLASSIFICATION OF CLOUDS

## Introduction

Cloud identification can be and often is, somewhat complicated, various types of clouds being present at different levels at the same time; on other occasions it may be quite simple with only one cloud type present. It is important that a seafarer should be able to recognise the main cloud types because of their bearing upon existing and future weather; he or she does not need to be a weather forecaster but the arrival of a particular type of cloud may confirm the timing of a particular forecast or may give warning of an unexpected weather change. This can be particularly useful when weather forecasts are for any reason unobtainable. A seafarer also needs to be able to recognise and name cloud types for inclusion in weather reports which are transmitted to a meteorological service. The cloud formation in any locality is an important feature of most weather situations and provides the meteorologist with valuable information when preparing a forecast.

## Summary of cloud types

The names and descriptions of the various cloud types have been agreed internationally by the World Meteorological Organisation. The earliest cloud classification, prepared in 1803, contained five types derived from Latin words – *cirrus* (meaning 'thread'), *cumulus* (heap), *stratus* (layer), *nimbus* (grey rain cloud) and *fractus* (broken). The present classification is an amplification and combination of these. Briefly, cirrus clouds are of a feathery or fibrous appearance; cumulus are cauliflower shaped above with a flattish base; stratus clouds form a more or less shapeless or homogenous layer or sheet; nimbus clouds have a uniform dark grey and threatening appearance, often with precipitation or 'virga' trailing beneath. Cloud types are further divided into three groups based upon their height above the observer: high, medium and low.

## Clouds heights

The names of the main cloud types, their abbreviations and their approximate heights are shown in the table below.

| CLOUD GROUP | AVERAGE HEIGHT RANGES (For middle latitudes) | CLOUDS |
|---|---|---|
| LOW LEVEL CLOUDS | From near surface level to about 2,000 metres (6,500 feet) | Stratus (St) Nimbostratus (Ns) Stratocumulus (Sc) |
| Clouds of marked vertical extent (heap clouds) | From near surface level to about 14,000 metres (45,000 feet) | Cumulus (Cu) Cumulonimbus (Cb) |
| MEDIUM LEVEL CLOUDS | About 2,000 metres (6,500 feet) to about 5,500 metres (18,000 feet) | Altocumulus (Ac) Altostratus (As) |
| HIGH LEVEL CLOUDS | About 5,500 metres (18,000 feet) to about 14,000 metres (45,000 feet) | Cirrus (Ci) Cirrocumulus (Cc) Cirrostratus (Cs) |

The abbreviations as shown above are customarily used by meteorologists and voluntary observers in describing the clouds.

## Description of cloud types (see photos 1 to 16)

### Stratus (St)

A more or less continuous layer or sheet of cloud, similar in appearance to fog but rarely touching the ground except in the case of high land. When it does touch the ground it is indistinguishable from fog. When broken up into patches by the wind it is called fractostratus (Fs). Height of base generally between 150 metres (500 feet) and 600 metres (2,000 feet).

### Nimbostratus (Ns)

A low, dark grey, shapeless and somewhat ragged cloud, of rainy appearance, often having below it pieces of 'scud' termed Fractostratus (Fs) from which precipitation may often fall; when it does it is usually continuous. Height of base is usually between 150 metres (500 feet) and 600 metres (2,000 feet) but may be either very close to the surface or is sometimes as high as 1,200 metres (4,000 feet).

## Stratocumulus (Sc)

An extensive layer or patches or rolls of globular shaped light grey clouds. They are often arranged in lines or groups orientated in one or two directions. When covering the whole sky they give it a wavy appearance. Height of base is usually between about 460 metres (1,500 feet) and 1,350 metres (4,500 feet). (See also altocumulus and cirrocumulus.)

## Cumulus (Cu)

Whitish cauliflower shaped clouds with a more or less flat base and appreciable vertical thickness. They vary in size and vertical extent and can develop up to great heights (see Cb). These clouds are a feature of the trade wind area – but can occur anywhere. In certain conditions of light, parts of these look dark. Base height is usually between about 460 metres (1,500 feet) and 1,500 metres (5,000 feet).

## Cumulonimbus (Cb)

The thundercloud, a cumulus type of cloud but of great vertical extent. The top, instead of being rounded like a cauliflower, looks more mountainous or may grow into the shape of a fibrous looking anvil. The base is generally flattish and often has fractostratus (Fs) clouds below it from which precipitation falls. If cumulonimbus cloud is very extensive it may resemble nimbostratus (Ns). Height of base is usually between 460 metres (1,500 feet) and 1,500 metres (5,000 feet).

## Altocumulus (Ac)

A layer or patches of flattish, globular shaped, fairly small clouds, white or grey in colour, often arranged in lines, very similar in appearance to stratocumulus but at a greater height and the individual cloudlets look smaller. Base height above 2,000 metres (6,500 feet) and not easy to estimate. (See also strato-cumulus and cirrocumulus.)

## Altostratus (As)

A thin and apparently formless veil or sheet of cloud, usually grey in colour. When present it often covers the whole sky, giving it a watery appearance; sun or moon shows through it with blurred outline. Sometimes it is thick enough to obscure sun or moon, in which case it is dark in colour. Base height above 2,000 metres (6,500 feet) and not easy to estimate. (See also cirrostratus.)

## Cirrus (Ci)

Nicknamed 'mares' tails', feathery, fibrous or hairy clouds of delicate texture, high in the sky, usually coloured white and in various formations. Height of base above about 5,500 metres (1,800 feet).

### Cirrocumulus (Cc)

Layers or patches of very small globular cloudlets similar in appearance to diminutive altocumulus but derived from cirrus clouds. Popularly known as 'mackerel sky', the cloudlets are arranged usually in lines and somewhat resemble flocks of sheep. Base height above about 5,500 metres (18,000 feet). (See also altocumulus and stratocumulus.)

### Cirrostratus (Cs)

A diffuse and thin veil of cloud, whitish in colour somewhat similar to altostratus, but more diffuse. Only slightly blurs the outline of the sun and moon; it often produces a halo effect which altostratus does not. Sometimes gives the sky a greyish or milky effect. Base height above about 5,500 metres (18,000 feet). (See altostratus.)

## Weather associated with cloud types

With a few obvious exceptions, a particular cloudscape does not indicate very much by itself about impending weather changes; it needs to be considered against a background of the process of formation or dissipation of those particular clouds, also the wind and pressure changes that have occurred recently. Ideally, a synoptic map is needed to get an overall picture of what is happening to the weather some distance away. It can be said, in very general terms, that at sea level the possible indications usually associated with certain cloud types are as follows, but complications may arise if high land is involved.

### Stratus

No special significance but may affect visibility if very low. Indicates a stable air mass, ie not much convection. Drizzle often falls from this cloud.

### Nimbostratus

Can be termed the rain cloud. Considerable rain probable and prospects of bad weather generally. In some cases the rain does not reach the ground.

### Stratocumulus

No special significance, not generally a bad weather cloud. As with stratus, it indicates stability. Occasionally light rain or drizzle falls from this cloud.

### Cumulus

Generally a fair weather cloud when small. When large they indicate unstable air with possibility of showers due to strong convection, and of sudden squally wind when nearby. If it thickens to windward it may indicate rain.

### Altocumulus

No special significance, not generally a bad weather cloud. Rain is likely when these clouds thicken to windward.

## Altostratus

Is not infrequently a herald of rain (and wind) and may give warning of an approaching depression if it derives from cirrostratus and is accompanied by a falling barometer.

## Cirrus

If it grows in extent it may well indicate the approach of windy and bad weather generally. Gives timely warning of a tropical storm, especially if followed by a falling barometer. If it turns to altostratus it probably indicates a coming depression or confirms the advent of a tropical storm. If it disperses it probably has no significance.

## Cirrocumulus

'Not long wet not long dry' seems a fair summary of its message, associated with fair weather and little wind.

## Cirrostratus

Gives a fair indication of the approach of rain. If it follows cirrus it may well indicate approach of a depression, or a tropical storm.

## QUESTIONS

1 (a) Name the ten principal cloud types and write their abbreviations.
   (b) Between what limiting heights are 'low', 'medium' (or 'middle') and 'high' clouds found?

2 Give a description of each of the following cloud types: Ci, Cs, As, Cb, Ns and Fs ('scud').

3 (a) What are mares' tails?
   (b) What might they indicate if they increase in density?

4 Describe the appearance of altostratus clouds. What does this type often portend?

5 Name the clouds associated with thunderstorms.

# 5 CLOUD FORMATION AND DEVELOPMENT

## Adiabatic heating and cooling

(*See Adiabatic in the Glossary.*)

When a body of air is subjected to an increase in pressure it undergoes compressional heating as opposed to thermal heating. If the same body of air is subjected to a reduction in pressure it undergoes expansional cooling as opposed to thermal cooling. For an example in the former case, the temperature of the air in a bicycle pump is increased when vigorously compressed. In the latter case, when compressed gas is released from a cylinder its temperature falls.

## Adiabatic processes in the atmosphere

Atmospheric pressure decreases with height. Thus if a body of air rises through the surrounding air (ie its environment) it undergoes a reduction in pressure and is cooled adiabatically. Conversely, if it sinks it is subjected to an increase in pressure and is warmed adiabatically. In both cases no interchange of heat takes place between the body of air and its environment.

## Cloud formation (in brief)

1 When unsaturated air is forced to rise it will expand and cool adiabatically.

2 If the ascent continues long enough it will reach its dew point and become saturated.

3 Further upward motion will result in the condensation of excess water vapour in the form of cloud (visible water droplets or, if the temperature is low enough, ice crystals).

*Note:* Moist air gives a relatively low cloud base, dry air a relatively high cloud base.

## Adiabatic lapse rates

*(See 'Lapse rate' in the Glossary.)*

### Dry adiabatic lapse rate (DALR)

When unsaturated air is forced to rise through its environment it cools at a **constant rate** of 1°C per 100 metres (5.4°F per 1,000 feet).

### Saturated adiabatic lapse rate (SALR)

Upward motion of saturated air results in condensation of excess water vapour. The process of condensation releases the latent heat of vaporisation which, in turn, warms the air around the water droplets thus reducing to some extent the expansional cooling. Hence the SALR is less than the DALR. See Figure 5. 1.

Near the Earth's surface the SALR averages about half the DALR, ie about 0.5°C per 100 metres (2.7°F per 1,000 feet). As the rising air gains height above the condensation level (see Glossary) the amount of water vapour is progressively reduced, so there is less and less condensation taking place and, therefore, less and less release of latent heat. Thus the SALR increases with height, but it can never exceed the DALR.

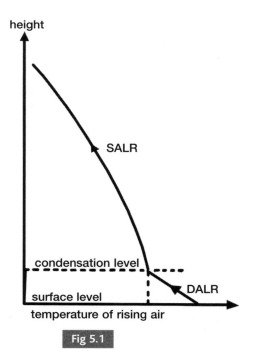

Fig 5.1

## The Environmental lapse rate (ELR)

The ELR within the troposphere averages about 0.6°C per 100 metres (1°F per 300 feet), but the actual value is subject to irregular variations with time, place and altitude. Refer now to Figure 5.2, which illustrates the characteristic shapes of four possible environmental temperature/height graphs (ELR curves):

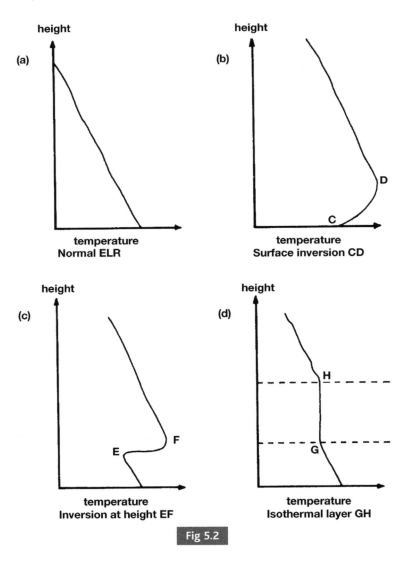

Fig 5.2

(a) Represents a near average ELR curve with some slight variations.

(b) Illustrates a curve with negative* lapse rate in the surface levels. A **surface inversion** may be caused through radiation cooling of a land surface at night, or by a warm air mass moving over a relatively very cold surface.

(c) Shows an **inversion at height** which may be brought about by dry air subsiding from upper levels and being warmed at the DALR during its descent. It is generally associated with an anticyclone, and this will be explained fully in Chapter 15.

(d) Illustrates an **isothermal layer** which, like the inversion at height, may be formed by the subsidence of dry air.

## Atmospheric stability and instability

(*See Stability in the Glossary.*)

If a body of air at the surface becomes warmer than the surrounding air it will commence to rise through the environment and, in so doing will cool adiabatically (see Figure 5.1). Upward motion will be arrested at the level where the temperature of the rising air reaches that of the environment. The height at which this takes place is governed almost entirely by the shape of the ELR curve.

Refer now to Figure 5.3 (a), (b) and (c). The Temperature/Height graphs $AE_1$, $GE_2$, and $CE_3$ represent three ELRs of different values, FD and BS the DALR and SALR respectively. Z represents a specimen of air at the level WX. It is important to note that, at any height, the temperature difference between an environmental curve and either one of the adiabatic curves is represented by the horizontal distance between the relevant curves.

### Case 1 Stable air (Figure 5.3a)

Assuming the existing ELR is $AE_1$:

a) If a vertical force causes the air specimen (Z) to rise it will, if unsaturated, cool at the DALR or, if saturated, at the SALR. The graph shows that the rising air at each successive level becomes progressively cooler (and therefore denser and heavier) than the surrounding air, thus increasing its initial resistance to upward motion.

If the displacing force ceases to act, the air specimen, being colder than its environment, will sink back to its original level (WX) where its temperature will be the same as that of its environment and it will offer resistance to any vertical displacement upwards or downwards.

---

* a negative temperature lapse rate (called an **inversion**) is one in which the air temperature increases with height.

b) Should the air specimen be initially forced downwards instead of upwards, it will warm adiabatically during descent, become lighter than the surrounding air and thus offer increasing resistance to its downward motion. If the displacing force should cease to act the air specimen will start to float upwards and finally come to rest at its original level.

## Case 2 Unstable air (Figure 5.3b)

In this case the ELR is greater than the DALR, a condition whereby the air is unstable regardless of whether it is saturated or dry. So we take, for example, the graph $GE_2$, as the existing ELR in the figure, and assume that a vertical force is applied to the air specimen (Z) for only long enough to displace it a small distance upwards.

a) During this initial movement the rising air, although cooling adiabatically, will become warmer and lighter than its environment (because both adiabatic curves lie to the right of the ELR). Thus the initial forced motion will be stimulated and the air will continue to rise after the displacing force has been removed.

b) If the initial displacing force acts downwards, the descending air will warm adiabatically but the graph will show that it becomes progressively cooler than its environment as height decreases. Thus the downward motion is stimulated and will continue after the displacing force ceases to act.

*Note:* In general, stratiform cloud is associated with stable air and cumuliform cloud with unstable air.

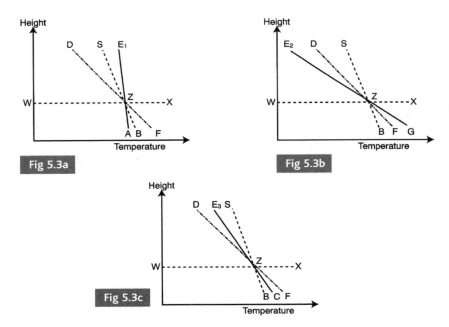

Fig 5.3a

Fig 5.3b

Fig 5.3c

**Photo 1** Cirrus

These long thread-like streaks of cloud are composed of tiny ice crystals. 'Mares' tails' is a common name because they look like the hairs of a horse's tail. When these clouds move quickly across the sky, becoming more dense, they may herald the approach of a depression. Watch how your barometer behaves from now on. *Photo by Mrs M I Holmes*

**Photo 2** | Cirrostratus

This cloud layer, visible in the upper part of the picture, is composed of ice crystals and sometimes appears in patches associated with other types of cirrus. When cirrostratus covers the sun or moon, a ring of light called a 'halo' is often visible. If cirrostratus increases to cover the whole sky it may foretell the approach of a depression. Watch for the appearance of altostratus with lowering base and falling barometer. *Photo by C S Broomfield*

**Photo 3** Cirrocumulus

This variety of cloud is not unlike altocumulus but the cloudlets are much higher, smaller and gleam whiter. The cloudlets often lie in ripples or lines and are then commonly described as 'Mackerel Sky'. Cirrocumulus is usually seen in association with patches of cirrus from which it often develops. The associated weather is usually fair and quiet and the cloud movement very slow. *Photo by W S Pike*

**Photo 4** Altostratus (thin)

Here the sky is covered with a featureless layer of cloud at medium levels. The cloud is thin enough for a watery sun or moon to be visible. When altostratus thickens to windward it may indicate the approach of a depression and, if so, a period of continuous rain soon begins. Watch your barometer. *Photo by R K Pilsbury*

**Photo 5** Altocumulus and cirrocumulus in bands

This cloud comprises individual elements. Here they completely cover the sky.
*Photo by S Jebson*

**Photo 6**  Altocumulus (stratified)

Here the cloud elements are at medium level. Sometimes several layers of this cloud type can be seen at different levels, one above the other. When altocumulus thickens to windward and loses its rounded shapes, a spell of dull rainy weather is likely. *Photo by R K Pilsbury*

**Photo 7** Stratus (layer)

When this grey featureless layer of low cloud covers the sky it is difficult to estimate the height of its base unless there are hills or cliffs nearby as in this case. Drizzle often falls from this cloud. *Photo by R K Pilsbury*

**Photo 8** | Stratocumulus

This soft-looking layer of cloud shows rolls or rounded masses beneath. These rolls or patches are often arranged in a fairly regular pattern of wavy lines or groups. Breaks are often visible in the cloud layer. Occasional light rain or drizzle sometimes falls from this cloud. *Photo by W S Pike*

**Photo 9** Nimbostratus with stratus fractus

This low level rainbearing cloud is thick enough to obscure the sun. The stratus fractus appears as ragged pieces of cloud below the main cloud layer. Nimbostratus is frequently associated with fronts. *Photo by C S Broomfield*

**Photo 10** Nimbostratus

Another example of this rain-bearing cloud linked with fronts. *Photo by C S Broomfield*

**Photo 11** Developing cumulus

These small, white, low clouds are developing in rising currents of air. If the clouds remain small, fine weather is likely to continue. *Photo by J F P Galvin*

**Photo 12** Cumulus

Small cumulus clouds sometimes continue to grow and develop into much larger masses with many towers or turrets. Their flat bases look dark by comparison with their gleaming white tops which are usually well rounded and often show a hard outline against a clear blue sky. When the tops begin to lose their rounded cauliflower-like appearance and become fibrous, showers can be expected. Cumulus clouds often tend to flatten out or disperse at sunset when convection ceases. *Photo by Cleo Irving*

**Photo 13** Cumulonimbus

Large cumulus clouds may develop further, extending from the base upwards to a height above the freezing level, where their tops are fibrous in appearance. With still further development their fibrous tops spread out like an anvil. Heavy showers of rain, snow or hail fall from these clouds, often accompanied by thunderstorms. Sudden hard squalls and a large change or reversal in wind direction may occur in the vicinity of well-developed cumulonimbus clouds. Such clouds often cover a wide area, especially when formed along a cold front.
*Photo © Crown*

**Photo 14** Sea fog

In this photo Arctic sea smoke can be clearly identified in Loch Linnhe. *Photo by J F P Galvin*

**Photo 15** Sea fog

This provides an excellent comparison with photo 14 as the sea smoke lifts.
*Photo by J F P Galvin*

**Photo 16** Orographic cloud

These clouds are produced by the airflow over hills or mountains and are sometimes referred to as wave clouds. The clouds in this picture resemble a pile of plates. Orographic cloud is continuously forming at the windward edge and evaporating downwind although it appears to be stationary. *Photo by R B Tucker*

## Case 3 Conditionally unstable air (Figure 5.3c)

In this case the value of the ELR lies between the DALR and the SALR and is represented by the curve CE₃ in the figure.

If the air at the height level WX is **saturated** it is **unstable** because the ELR is less than the SALR but if it is **unsaturated** it is **stable** because the ELR is greater than the DALR.

The degree of stability or instability depends not only on the shape of the ELR curve but also on the height of the condensation level which is governed by the dew point.

Refer now to Figures 5.4(a) and 5.4(b), in each of which the letter T represents the air temperature at surface level, V the temperature to which a sample of surface air is raised by solar radiation, and D the dew point of the air. Note that the values of T, V and the ELR are the same in both figures, but D is different.

First now consider Figure 5.4(a). The air specimen of temperature V will rise through its environment cooling at the DALR until it reaches its dew point at the condensation level (CL) at which height it is saturated and, being still warmer than the surrounding air, will continue to rise but now cooling at the SALR, and so becoming increasingly unstable. The cloud thus formed could reach to a very great height.

Comparing Figures 5.4(a) and 5.4(b), it is clearly shown that although the values of T, V and the ELR remain unchanged, in Figure 5.4(b) the dew point (D) is relatively low hence the condensation level (CL) is relatively high. In this

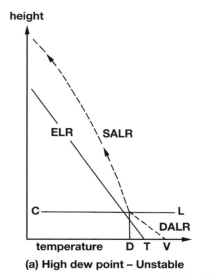

**(a) High dew point – Unstable**

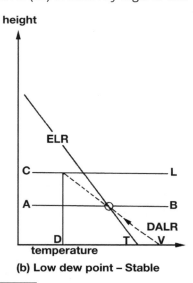

**(b) Low dew point – Stable**

Fig 5.4 (a) and (b)

example the specimen of warmed air, rising and cooling at the DALR reaches the same temperature as that of its environment at the level AB where all upward motion is arrested. Thus the air becomes stable at a height well below that of the condensation level and cloud cannot form.

Figure 5.5 illustrates an intermediate condition whereby, although the rising air is unstable at the condensation level, it becomes stable when it has gained sufficient height. This is because the SALR increases with altitude and the curve eventually meets that of the ELR at a level at which upward motion of air ceases and is thus the maximum height to which cloud can develop.

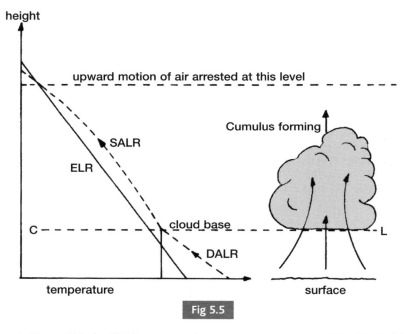

**Fig 5.5**

In Figure 5.6 the ELR is greater than average up to a considerable height. Surface heating by the sun is strong and the dew point is high. The atmosphere is thus very unstable. Under these conditions cloud of great vertical develop-ment can be expected.

Figure 5.7 illustrates a subsidence inversion above the condensation level (CL). All upward motion of air will be arrested at the level of the inversion (QR). Layer type cloud will be formed; if the base is below 300 metres it will be stratus. A higher base gives stratocumulus.

If the dew point is *low* enough to give a condensation level above QR the sky will be cloudless. See Figure 5.8.

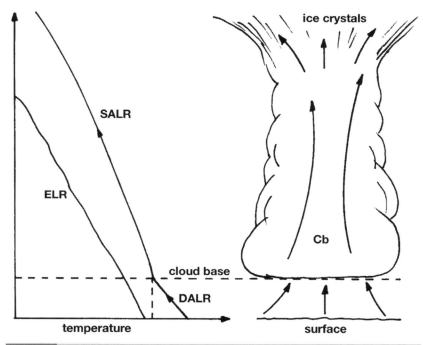

**Fig 5.6** *Unstable atmosphere.*

In stable atmosphere the cloud formed will be stratiform. Very moist air gives low stratus. Fairly dry air gives a higher, smoother cloud base – stratocumulus. See Photos 7 and 8.

In unstable atmosphere cloud will be cumuliform. The greater the degree of instability the greater the amount of cumuliform cloud.

## Main causes of initial uplift of air

1 **Thermal uplift** has been described earlier in this chapter and is the result of the air temperature being raised through contact with a warmer surface.

2 **Turbulent uplift.** Air flowing horizontally over a rough surface sets up horizontal and vertical eddy currents which occur mainly in the lowest 600 metres of the troposphere. The actual height to which this turbulence can extend depends on the nature of the surface and the force of the wind. When surface air is forced up to a height above the condensation level cloud will form. Turbulence can occur from a variety of causes anywhere in the troposphere. It gives altocumulus cloud at medium heights and cirrocumulus at high levels.

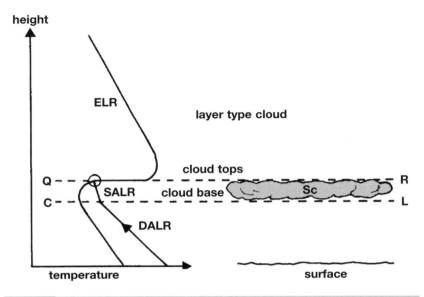

**Fig 5.7** *Stable atmosphere.*

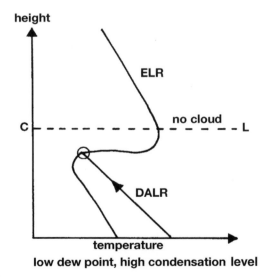

low dew point, high condensation level

**Fig 5.8** *Stable atmosphere.*

3 **Orographic uplift** occurs when an airstream meets an obstructing coastline or barrier of hills and is forced upwards irrespective of whether the air is stable or unstable. Cloud will not form unless the air is lifted above the condensation level. Orographic cloud can be either stratiform or cumuliform depending on whether the rising air is stable or unstable after passing the condensation level.

A very well known orographic stratus cloud is the 'tablecloth' which often forms on Table Mountain, Cape Town, when warm moist air flows in from over the sea. This cloud covers the flat table 'top' and appears to hang down on the lee side for some distance, till the descending air causes evaporation after adiabatic warming. A similar effect sometimes occurs at Gibraltar.

Orographic uplift of warm moist air can produce very heavy rain, much of which is deposited on the windward slopes of the obstructing hills or mountains. In such cases the weather on the lee side is relatively warm and dry. For example, with a westerly airstream flowing across Scotland, giving cold wet weather on the West Coast, it is not uncommon to have mild dry weather on the East Coast. This is called a 'Föhn effect' (See **Föhn** and **Chinook** in Glossary.)

4 **Frontal uplift** operates mainly within depressions but can occur elsewhere. More often than not the cloud structures of the warm front are of layer type, whereas cumuliform cloud is a common feature of the cold front. Frontal uplift is fully explained in Chapter 13.

5 **Uplift resulting from convergent winds.** When the horizontal inflow of air into an area exceeds the horizontal outflow, the surface air is forced upwards mechanically. Except in arid regions convergence is generally associated with much cloud and precipitation; typical examples are at fronts and centres of depressions.

## QUESTIONS

1 Define the following terms: water vapour, relative humidity, dew point, saturated air, unsaturated air, condensation and convection.

2 What are hygroscopic nuclei and how are they related to the process of condensation in the atmosphere?

3 **Adiabatic lapse rates**
Distinguish between thermal and dynamical changes of temperature in the atmosphere.

4 The SALR averages about half the value of the DALR near the Earth's surface.
(a) What is the value of the DALR?
(b) Explain why the SALR increases with height and why it can never exceed the DALR.

5 **Environmental lapse rates**
(a) What is the average ELR within the troposphere?
(b) What is a surface inversion? Describe two situations in which it is commonly formed.

6 How is an inversion at height brought about?

7 What is an isothermal layer?

8 Cloud formation. Name and describe the five main modes of initial uplift of air.

9 Summarise the physical processes which result in cloud formation.

10 **Atmospheric stability and instability**
Draw simple temperature v height graphs to illustrate stable and unstable air. (Values for temperature and height are not required.) State what cloud types are associated with each.

11 Given a situation in which the atmosphere is conditionally unstable, what are the three factors which together determine the degree of stability or instability?

# 6 PRECIPITATION

In meteorology '**precipitation**' is a generic word embracing most forms of water deposit which are derived from the condensation of water vapour in the atmosphere. It includes rain, drizzle, snow, sleet and hail which, together, are the more common concept of the term; but it also includes dew, hoar frost, rime and glazed frost which are, more often than not, regarded by mariners as 'not strictly precipitation'. Meteorologists refer to all of these phenomena as **hydrometeors**.

Cloud, fog and mist are not classed as precipitation but are hydrometeors.

The difference between **rain** and **drizzle** is only that the drops in drizzle are relatively very small (diameter between 0.2 and 0.5 millimetres) and light. They fall slowly and gently from low based stratus cloud. Unless the relative humidity is high beneath the cloud base the drops are likely to evaporate before reaching the surface.

## Rain and drizzle

### Formation

Raindrops vary in size but they are all larger than the tiny droplets or ice particles of which clouds are composed; to turn these into rain appreciable convection (vertical movement) within the cloud is necessary. When convection is active within cloud the water droplets are carried up to greater heights and the process of cooling and condensation continues. A proportion of the droplets will increase in size due to either:

❖ Collision and coalescence of very small droplets with larger ones, and/or
❖ Growth of ice crystals at the expense of water droplets, in clouds where ice crystals and water droplets initially co-exist.

Whatever the formation process rain is nearly always created in clouds of appreciable vertical extent. The greater the vertical thickness of the cloud the larger the raindrops. Thus drizzle may fall from quite shallow cloud.

When the droplets are large and heavy enough to overcome the upward motion of air they will commence to fall. During descent through cloud they will continue to increase in size due to collision with the rising cloud droplets, until they fall as rain from the base of the cloud.

Some evaporation takes place in the warmer unsaturated air below the cloud base; if the falling drops are large enough in both size and number they will reach the surface.

The dark vertical or trailing streaks of precipitation seen falling from the base of a cloud, and which do not reach the surface, are called **virga** or **fallstreaks**.

## Classification of rain

There are three main types:

### 1 Convectional rain

Associated with unstable atmosphere, high relative humidity, and a large lapse rate in the lower levels due to strong solar heating of a land surface, particularly during the hottest hours of the day.

Sea surface temperatures undergo very little change in temperature during the course of a day (see Chapter 2), but moisture-laden air moving over a relatively very warm sea surface will often produce convectional rain, usually in the form of isolated showers, sometimes heavy with hail and thunder, especially in tropical regions.

### 2 Orographic rain

This occurs when a moisture-laden airstream encounters a range of hills or mountains, and is thus forced to rise to heights well above the condensation level. It is usually heaviest on the weather slopes and may be very light or negligible on the leeward side. (See Föhn in Glossary.)

This type of rain can be exceptionally heavy and persistent if given suitable conditions: for example, the Western Ghats of India (height about 1900 metres); during the south-west monsoon the very heavy rain is almost continuous for three months but is comparatively slight on the leeward side.

When sea winds cross a coast, surface friction on forested land is considerable and forms a barrier of air over which the oncoming air is forced to rise and sometimes causes precipitation.

### 3 Frontal rain

This is associated mainly with depressions of the temperate latitudes. Details are given in Chapter 13.

## Snow and sleet

### Formation

When water vapour condenses at temperatures well below freezing point it forms minute ice crystals which, during their very slow fall through cloud, build up a growth of feathery crystals forming **snowflakes**.

The size of snowflakes depends on temperature. In very low temperatures the ice crystals do not unite to form snowflakes, but may do so on reaching lower levels of the cloud where the temperatures are less cold. Thus the lower the temperature the smaller the snow flakes which reach the surface.

For snow to reach the ground, air temperature near the surface must be lower than 3.5°C (38°F). Above about 3°C (37°F) it will fall as **sleet** which is a mixture of snow and rain or of melting snow. Whether the snow lies or not depends mainly on the temperature of the surface on which it falls.

In very cold weather heavy snowfall can adversely affect a ship's stability. Heavy snow can also seriously affect visibility.

## Hail

Hail falls from **cumulonimbus cloud** in the form of hard ice pellets of varying shapes and is often associated with thunderstorms.

### Formation

Vigorous convection currents may carry **supercooled water drops** (see Glossary) up to a height where ice crystals are present and are supported by strong updrafts. The ice particles grow in size by collision and coalescence with the supercooled water drops which freeze instantly on impact thereby forming pellets of white opaque ice (called soft hail). When the pellets become large enough they will commence to fall and continue to grow.

On entering the lower levels of the cloud where the temperature may be a little above 0°C (32°F) they may encounter water drops which are not supercooled and which freeze *slowly* on to the freezing hailstones surrounding them with a coating of hard *clear ice* before they fall below the cloud base.

Due to the strong turbulent eddies, which are a characteristic of cumulonimbus clouds, some hailstones make several upward and downward journeys between the upper and lower levels of the cloud before finally falling to earth. This would account for the concentric structure of very large hailstones which when cut in half may be seen to be made up of alternate layers of opaque and clear ice.

In winter when the freezing level is well below the cloud base, above which all water drops must be supercooled, there will be no coating of clear ice on the hailstones.

## Size of hailstones

On reaching the surface the size of hailstones depends mainly on the vertical extent of the cloud in which they are formed and the strength of the upcurrents within it. Usually they measure only a few millimetres in diameter. In some hot, moist regions of the world hailstones larger than cricket balls and weighing 1 to 2 kg have been reported.

## *Glazed frost*

This, as the name suggests, is a layer of ice which looks like glass. It occurs when surface temperatures are below 0°C (32°F) often at the end of a severe 'cold spell'.

Rain or drizzle falling from the cloud associated with a warm front will freeze immediately on contact with the cold surface and other cold objects, coating everything with smooth clear ice.

This form of ice can also be produced by fog droplets freezing onto cold objects. The term 'black ice' is also used to describe a thin coating of this ice on a road surface, the temperature of which is below 0°C. It is occasionally confused with black frost (see Glossary).

## *Sea spray*

The most dangerous form of icing encountered at sea is produced by sea spray freezing onto the vessel. Ice from this source can accumulate very rapidly and can pose a severe threat to stability, particularly of small vessels. The added weight will reduce a vessel's freeboard and make her 'top heavy', in addition to problems with lifesaving appliances, antennae and other equipment becoming frozen.

Sea water freezes at about −2°C (28.5°F). If the air temperature is below this, sea spray landing on the superstructure will freeze, producing a coating of ice. Significant amounts of spray are not generally present until wind speed reaches Force 5 and the rate of icing increases with increasing wind speed above this force.

## *Dew*

A deposit of water formed by condensation on surfaces which have been cooled by radiation to a temperature below that of the dew point of the air. Favourable conditions are a calm night with a clear sky and high relative humidity.

**A good example of ice accretion.** *Photo by J F Thomson*

## Hoar frost

A deposit of thin ice crystals or frozen dew upon surfaces whose temperatures have fallen below both dew point and 0°C.

## Rime

When suspected water droplets of fog strike solid objects such as trees, telephone wires, ship's masts, rigging and superstructure, at temperatures below 0°C they freeze on impact, forming a deposit of white ice crystals. The deposit is rough in appearance and grows to windward of the object.

# 7 THUNDERSTORMS

A thunderstorm is one of the more spectacular shows put on by nature. Its potential dangers to the mariner are its sometimes torrential rain, which may reduce visibility to zero; sudden squalls of wind; its risk of interference with radio communications (known as 'atmospherics' or 'static'); and the possibility of damage to magnetic compasses if the ship is struck by lightning (a rare event). The causes of a thunderstorm's formation are such that in general it is more violent when the weather is relatively warm and humid. In the Mediterranean, for example, a violent thunderstorm may last for an hour or two, creating serious difficulties for any ship trying to enter harbour and quite dangerous to a small vessel, especially if she is under sail. In temperate zones thunderstorms may occur at any time of the year during the passage of a cold front, due to cold air undercutting warmer air, but that tends to be a squally occasion in any case.

## Causes of thunderstorms

The conditions necessary for the formation of thunderstorms are:

- ❖ Cumulonimbus cloud with precipitation and the base below the 0°C isotherm.
- ❖ The lapse rate must exceed the saturated adiabatic to a height of at least 3,000 metres (10,000 feet) above the cloud base, thus facilitating vigorous convection.
- ❖ An adequate supply of moisture from below to facilitate this. The latent heat released by condensation within the cloud boosts the upward convection.

In temperate latitudes these conditions are most likely to be found in cols and shallow depressions, but the thunderstorms which result are not as frequent or violent as those which occur in the tropics.

Given the necessary conditions, as above, other favourable conditions are:

* High surface temperature.
* Little surface wind.
* 'Trigger action', such as:
  (a) Horizontal convergence of surface air.
  (b) Orographic uplift of moist air.
  (c) Frontal uplift, eg a cold front.
  (d) Insolation over land.
  (e) Advective heating or
  (f) Any combination of the above.

## Heavy rain and hail

The formation of hail is described in Chapter 6; the very heavy nature of the rain, which is also a frequent feature of thunderstorms, is due to somewhat similar processes within the cumulonimbus cloud. Hail and heavy rain, although often present within the cumulonimbus cloud, do not necessarily reach the ground on all occasions.

## Lightning and thunder

The intense activity within a Cb cloud results in the build up of tremendous electrical charges. Scientific investigations have shown that the upper part of a thunder cloud is charged with positive electricity, lower down the charge is negative. Near the base there is often a small localised region which is positive.

### Lightning flash

This is an electric spark on a gigantic scale, ie an enormous electrical discharge (estimated to be millions of volts) which takes place either within the thunder cloud, between two separate clouds, or between cloud and earth. It renders the air white hot along its channel.

### Danger from lightning

The risk of a steel ship being struck by lightning is not very great because her masts and other prominent features, being part of her structure, are so perfectly earthed to the water in which she is floating. Ashore, the risk to high buildings and other erections not fitted with lightning conductors and to trees, is greater.

### Thunder

The sound resulting from the instantaneous expansion and contraction of the air is known as thunder. The rumbling effect which we hear is because the sound of the explosive report has to travel from different parts of the long lightning path to the observer and there may be echoes from the clouds.

Light travels very rapidly and can be treated as though it arrived instantaneously, but the sound travels at 335 metres per second (1,100 feet per second). The distance to a thunderstorm can be approximated by measuring the time in seconds between seeing the flash of light and the arrival of the sound. The distance in miles is found by dividing this figure by 5 and the distance in kilometres is found by dividing the figure by 3.

When the lightning stroke takes place between cloud and earth, or across a clear space between two clouds, its main channel (and 'branches') is directly visible to the eye and is called **forked lightning**, but when the channel is obscured by cloud, so that the emitted light is diffused, it is termed **sheet lightning**.

There are various theories as to the mechanism resulting in the separation of charges within a Cb cloud. Most of them have good experimental support but it is thought that several of the charging processes operate together and, in addition, there are other electrical processes which are not yet completely understood.

## Types of thunderstorm

### Heat thunderstorms

These develop over land in warm, moist conditions accompanied by strong surface heating and convection. Surface air flows in from all sides (thus, to an observer positioned in advance of the storm, it would appear to be travelling against the wind). In temperate latitudes they are most frequent in summer, on late afternoons or evenings of warm sultry days with light winds. Mountainous islands in the tropics are especially prone to these.

### Coastal thunderstorms

This type can occur in any season, by day or night. They are most frequent in winter and are caused by a large lapse rate in polar maritime air. The final 'trigger action' comes from the forced ascent of air crossing the coast from seaward. They are usually slight and dissipate rapidly on moving inland.

### Frontal thunderstorms

More common in winter in temperate latitudes, frontal thunderstorms occur because there are more depressions at that time.

**Active cold fronts** are unstable, especially when there is a large temperature difference between the warm and cold air masses and if the frontal convergence is extremely marked, as for example in a V-shaped trough (see Line squall in Glossary).

**Warm front thunderstorms** are uncommon and less active, because the frontal slope is gradual. They form at upper levels which leaves little room for development of Cb cloud. (Compare Figures 13.12 and 13.13.)

**Occlusions** sometimes produce thunderstorms, more often with cold occlusions than with warm ones.

## General

Thunderstorms over the ocean. Except in the doldrums only the frontal type are experienced. They are rare in high latitudes due to low temperatures and consequent lack of moisture.

At night it is possible, over land or sea, for severe thunderstorms to develop given favourable conditions aloft, but some initial 'trigger action' is required to start the cloud formation.

Passage of a thunderstorm is associated with a sudden fall in temperature, which can be of the order of 10°C or 11°C. This is due to cold air from high level being dragged down to the surface by falling precipitation. The precipitation is localised and may be very heavy. The arrival of the cold air is associated with a sudden veer in wind direction with a fierce squall and there are violent squalls with large changes in wind direction as the storm passes. The pressure generally rises at the forward edge of the storm and then there is a 'wake low' at the rear of the storm.

### QUESTIONS

1 (a) What are the three conditions essential for the development of a thunderstorm?
  (b) Name the pressure systems in which these conditions are most likely to be found in the middle latitudes.

2 Given the essential conditions required in Question 1(a), list other conditions which are favourable for thunderstorm development.

3 Name the three types of thunderstorm and discuss the conditions and time of day in which each is most likely to develop, also their seasons of greater frequency.

# 8 VISIBILITY

## General characteristics

### Bad visibility

Bad visibility may be due to the presence in the air of:

(a) visible moisture in the form of liquid water droplets (not water vapour, which is invisible) or

(b) solid particles such as dust, smoke or sea salt.

### Good visibility

Good visibility is favoured by air temperatures which are below that of the underlying surface and by strong winds.

### Terminology

When the horizontal visibility lies between 1,000 and 2,000 metres the terms **mist** or **haze** are used – the former only when the atmospheric obscurity is due to the presence of moisture and the latter when due to solid particles. The term **fog** is applied when the visibility, irrespective of cause, is below 1,000 metres (about 0.5 nautical mile).

### Formation of fog

Fog is formed by the cooling of a large volume of air below its dew point, resulting in condensation, a process similar to that of cloud formation but taking place at or near the sea or ground surface. In certain circumstances it may also be caused by the evaporation of water vapour into the air. The necessary cooling referred to above is caused by:

(a) proximity to cold land or sea and

(b) some turbulent mixing of the air.

## Types of fog

In order of the most likely frequency at sea, the principal types of fog are:

❖ Advection or sea fog
❖ Frontal fog
❖ Radiation fog
❖ Arctic sea smoke

## Advection fog

This is the most widespread type likely to be encountered at sea and is caused by relatively warm air being cooled by flowing over a cooler sea surface. The latter will be below the dew point of the air and normally the wind speed will be between 4 and 16 knots (between Force 2 and 4 on the Beaufort scale). There are only certain localities where such conditions are relatively prevalent. One is off the Grand Banks of Newfoundland where the cold Labrador Current causes a decrease in sea temperature. The warm, moist, southerly airstream flowing over this is cooled below its dew point to form advection, or sea fog.

The English Channel is often affected by advection fog when south-westerly winds reach the British Isles from the Azores in spring and early summer.

In ocean regions, well away from shallows and coastal waters, the sea surface temperature changes very little through solar heating or night radiation. Generally the daily change in sea surface temperature is less than 0.5°C.

It is possible to estimate the likelihood of the formation of fog from observations of air temperatures, wind direction and other weather signs, plus a knowledge of sea temperatures to be expected on the course ahead. Admiralty Ocean Routeing Charts give information for each month of the year on:

❖ Mean sea temperatures
❖ Mean dew point temperatures
❖ Percentage frequency of fog (visibility – less than half a mile)
❖ Percentage frequency of low visibility (less than 5 miles)
❖ Mean air temperatures
❖ Mean barometric pressures

## Frontal or mixing fog

This may occur along the boundary when two widely differing air masses meet. Usually associated with either a warm front or a warm occlusion when cold air meets warm moist air; hence it is normally experienced in temperate or high latitudes. It is caused by the evaporation of relatively warm rain or drizzle which in turn cools the air through which it falls.

## Radiation fog

This forms over land, most frequently during autumn and winter over low-lying land, especially if it is damp and marshy and in valleys on quiet nights with clear skies. Under these conditions the land loses heat by radiation and cools the air close to the ground, possibly to below its dew point. If there is a gentle breeze blowing (up to 5 knots), this will cause turbulent mixing but only close to the surface and condensation in the form of fog will take place. A stronger wind will cause the cooling to be diffused through a greater depth of air and the dew point will not be reached.

Since cold air is heavier than warm air, it will tend to drain down into valleys. Although it never actually forms over the sea, it may drift from the land for several miles but seldom extends for more than 10 miles offshore.

Cloudy skies overnight will reduce the effect of the radiation from the land, or even re-radiate heat back to the surface and radiation fog will not occur under these conditions.

Radiation fog will be most dense around sunrise and normally disperses fairly rapidly as the land warms.

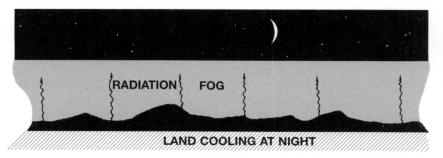

RADIATION FOG

LAND COOLING AT NIGHT

Fig 8.1

## Arctic sea smoke

This is a type of fog occurring close to the sea surface when the air is dry and cold – probably at least 9°C below the sea surface temperature. Rapid evaporation takes place from the relatively warm sea surface into the colder air and condensation takes place, giving the effect of steam or smoke rising from the sea.

It is most common in Arctic and Antarctic waters and in the Baltic but it can also occur off the eastern coasts of continents in winter, eg off Newfoundland and over inland seas and lakes. This is one type of fog which may also be associated with strong winds since it requires a continual supply of cold air.

## Mist, dust and haze

Visibility which is impaired but is more than 1,000 metres is described as mist – when caused by water droplets and when the relative humidity is more than 95%. When caused by smoke or dust particles it is described as haze.

Causes of the latter range from forest fires, smoke from industrial areas, to dust or sand storms which may be experienced to seaward of desert regions such as off the West African coast or off the Arabian coast when seasonal winds blow off the land.

Sand storms may extend up to 100 miles out to sea and constitute a serious problem for the mariner.

## Sound signals in fog

The very conditions which create fog may also cause distortions in both the direction from which another ship's fog signal appears to come and in its strength. The watchkeeper must therefore exercise considerable caution when attempting to estimate either the distance from another sound source or its direction.

## Use of radar in fog

Meteorological factors may affect the normal expected range of radars. If humidity decreases with height, super-refraction may be expected, resulting in a considerable increase in radar range. On the other hand, if humidity increases with height, sub-refraction may be expected with a consequent decrease in range.

Radar range is likely to be more adversely affected by heavy rain than by fog. It is recommended that further reference is made to the appropriate chapter of a specialist textbook dealing with radar.

## QUESTIONS

1  Differentiate between fog, mist and haze.

2  What are the necessary conditions for the formation of fog?

3  Good visibility is favoured by a large lapse rate and strong winds. Why is this so?

4  Describe the conditions which are most favourable for the formation of radiation fog.

5  (a) In which seasons does radiation fog most frequently occur? Explain why.
   (b) How may radiation fog affect the mariner?

6  At what time of day is radiation fog likely to be most intense? Explain why.

7  Describe the nature and topography of the surface which is most favourable for the formation and persistence of radiation fog.

8  Discuss the effects of smoke on visibility.

9  Define the term 'advection'.

10  What are the conditions necessary for the formation of advection fog?

11  What is the cause of Arctic sea smoke?

# 9 ATMOSPHERIC PRESSURE AND WIND

## Atmospheric pressure

Atmospheric pressure at any level (height above the sea) is caused by the weight of air which lies above that level. It follows, therefore, that pressure decreases as height increases; for example, atmospheric pressure at a height of approximately 5,500 metres (18,000 feet) is generally about half its value at ground level.

Surface pressure at any one point varies continually, the average is about 1,012 hPa at sea level.

### Units of barometric pressure

Pressure may be expressed in 'inches' or 'centimetres', being the equivalent to the height of a column of mercury (under certain standard conditions) which is required to balance atmospheric pressure. In modern meteorology pressure is expressed in hPa or millibars.

### Isobars

An isobar is a line, drawn on a weather chart, which passes through all points of equal barometric pressure. Isobars are spaced at intervals of one or more hPa, depending on the scale of the chart. The isobaric patterns which they form enable us to recognise definite pressure systems such as depressions, anticyclones, ridges, etc, each of which is associated with its own characteristic weather.

## Cause of wind

It is important at this stage to remember that atmospheric pressure at any point is exerted equally in all directions. (Unlike the force of gravity which acts vertically downwards.)

Horizontal movement of the air is caused by differences in pressure between one point at that level and another. This difference in pressure produces a *pressure gradient force*, which acts to move the air directly from high pressure to low pressure.

### Relationship between wind direction and isobars

The horizontal pressure gradient force acts at right angles to the isobars, but it is not the only force acting upon the air. The Earth is rotating upon its axis and this produces an effect upon the motion of the air which is seen by an observer at the Earth's surface. The path of the air appears to be deflected to the right in the northern hemisphere and to the left in the southern hemisphere. Calculation of this effect is simplified by using an imaginary force, the Coriolis force, to represent the effect of the Earth's rotation.

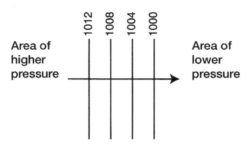

The arrow indicates the direction
of the pressure gradient force

Fig 9.1

At heights of 600 metres or more above the Earth's surface the effects of surface friction can be ignored. If the isobars are straight and parallel, the pressure gradient force is balanced by the Coriolis force and the geostrophic wind blows parallel to the isobars (see Figure 9.2).

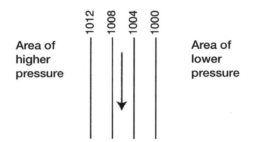

The arrow indicates the direction
of the geostrophic wind in the
northern hemisphere

Fig 9.2

## Buys Ballot's Law

If, in the northern hemisphere, an observer faces the wind, pressure is lower on his right hand than on his left (see Figure 9.2) whilst the converse is true in the southern hemisphere.

In latitudes within 5° of the equator the Earth's rotation is not effective, the wind flows straight across the isobars and Buys Ballot's Law does not apply.

## Relationship between pressure gradient and wind speed

The pressure gradient is the change in pressure with distance, where the distance is measured perpendicular to the isobars. The greater the pressure gradient the closer the isobars and the stronger the wind. Pressure gradient is described as steep when the isobars are close together and slack when they are widely spaced.

## The geostrophic wind speed

This may be found by means of a geostrophic wind scale printed on a synoptic weather chart, or else by means of a scale engraved on transparent plastic.

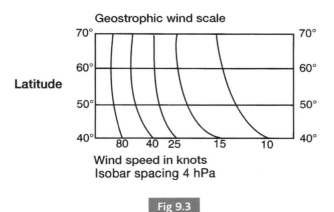

**Geostrophic wind scale**

Fig 9.3

The perpendicular distance between two isobars is measured and this distance laid off from the left-hand edge of the scale at the appropriate latitude. The geostrophic wind speed is found from the curved lines.

## The gradient wind

This wind flows parallel to curved isobars. A resultant force is needed to allow the air to travel on a curved path, so that now pressure gradient force and Coriolis force are not exactly equal. This results in the gradient wind speed being less than the geostrophic wind speed when circulating around low pressure and more than geostrophic when circulating around high pressure.

At the surface the angle between the wind and the isobars varies with the nature of the surface over which the wind blows; it may generally be taken as about 10° to 15° over the sea.

### Diurnal variation of wind speed at the surface

This is caused by diurnal variation in convection currents. During the day, when convection currents are strongest, the retarding effect of surface friction is diffused through a greater depth of turbulence (see Friction layer in Glossary). Thus the reduction in surface wind force is less by day. At night, when the depth of turbulence is shallow, the retarding effect is greater and therefore the wind force is less. The diurnal variation of wind speed over sea areas is negligible.

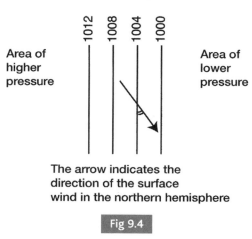

The arrow indicates the
direction of the surface
wind in the northern hemisphere

Fig 9.4

## Effect of temperature on surface pressure

A knowledge of the following will greatly assist in the understanding and memorising of the prevailing and seasonal winds of the world.

### Unequal heating of the Earth's surface

During the course of a year, sea surface temperatures change very little by comparison with land surfaces (especially in the interior of the continents). In the middle latitudes in summer the land becomes warmer than the surrounding sea, whereas in winter land temperatures are generally below that of the adjacent sea. This is because the specific heat capacity of water is higher than that of land.

If an area, such as a large land mass, is subjected to a long period of surface heating the air column above the area attains a mean temperature greater than that of its environment. Pressure at an upper level within the column then becomes higher than in the surrounding air at the same upper level.

At this upper level, air tends to flow away from the high pressure area towards cooler regions.

This reduces the total quantity of air over the warm area and so causes pressure to fall at the surface (less air, less weight and therefore less pressure). Similarly an inflow of air into an upper level of a cold region will cause surface pressure to rise. (See Figure 9.5.)

The continent of Asia shows a very marked example of the above. Surface pressure is low over north-west India in summer and very high over Siberia in winter. (See Monsoon in Glossary.)

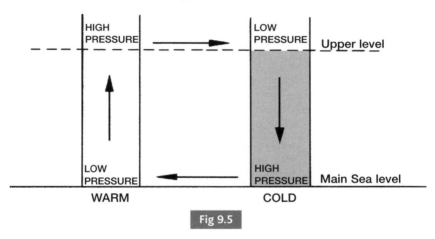

Fig 9.5

## Planetary system of pressure and winds

Within the tropics the sun's rays are nearly vertical throughout the whole of the year. At the polar caps they are nearly horizontal during the half-year that the sun is above the horizon. Thus surface heating is strong in equatorial latitudes and very weak in polar regions. (See Figure 9.6.)

### Idealised pressure distribution and wind circulation on a uniform globe

If the surface of the Earth were uniform, eg completely covered by water, belts of high pressure would develop in some latitudes, such as polar regions and belts of low pressure would develop in others, such as equatorial latitudes. The air moving towards the areas of lower pressure would be deflected due to the Coriolis force.

The 'idealised' pressure distribution and surface wind flow is shown in Figure 9.7.

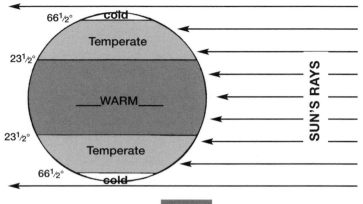

Fig 9.6

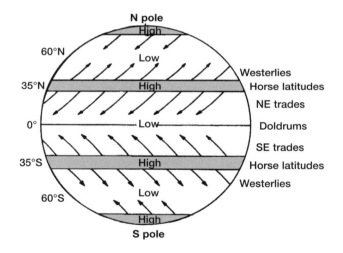

Fig 9.7

### Wind circulation on the Earth

The idealised wind pattern illustrated in Figure 9.7 is modified in practice due to the presence of the continental land masses, since there are large seasonal temperature variations over the continents. The modification is more significant in the northern hemisphere. The southern hemisphere has a small total land area in comparison to the great expanse of ocean and the wind circulation more nearly conforms to the ideal pattern.

## World pressure distribution and prevailing winds

Figures 9.8 and 9.9 show the mean distribution of Mean Sea Level (MSL) pressure for the months of January and July. The subtropical high pressure belts, though much broken up in the summer by land masses, are still clearly recognisable in both figures, with the highs lying towards the eastern sides of the oceans. These oceanic highs move north and south a little, following the annual movement of the sun. Take special note of the seasonal changes over Asia and compare the general flow of isobars in the North Indian Ocean with the North Atlantic and North Pacific. Bear in mind that Figures 9.8 and 9.9 show mean pressures for their respective months and that the pressure distribution locally on any particular day may show isobaric patterns very different from those illustrated.

## The prevailing winds of the oceans

The prevailing winds of the oceans conform to the main flow of isobars for the season and follow Buys Ballot's Law. The winds, especially in the southern hemisphere, show a similarity to those described for the uniform globe. They are, however, only mean winds and considerable variations can be expected locally from time to time. Ignoring, for the moment, the prevailing winds of the Indian Ocean, there is a definite clockwise circulation round the highs of the North Pacific and North Atlantic, and an anticlockwise circulation in the South Pacific and South Atlantic. The surface outflow of air from these highs produces the NE Trades and the SE Trades on their equatorial sides; westerly winds prevail on the poleward sides. In the central areas of these anticyclones light variable winds and calms with fine, clear weather generally persist. Vessels which are dependent only on sail for their propulsion can be delayed for long periods in these regions. (See Figures 9.10 and 9.11.)

### Trade winds

The Trade winds blow more or less constantly (except when monsoons prevail) throughout all seasons at a mean speed of around 14 knots and are generally strongest in the late winter. They extend from about latitude 30° towards the equator and change their direction gradually with the curvature of the isobars. The Trade wind areas follow slightly the annual movement of the sun. Note,

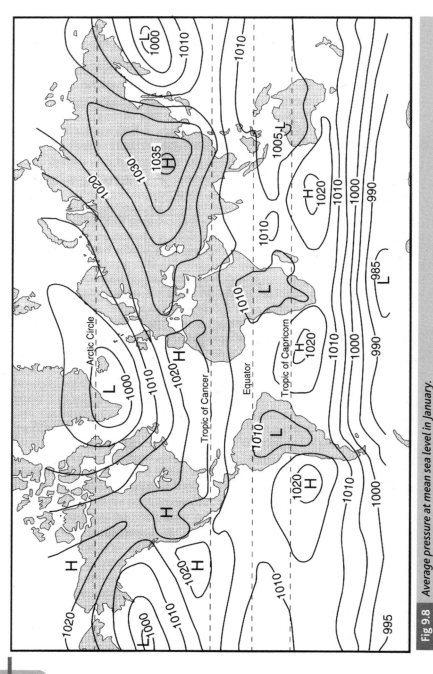

**Fig 9.8** *Average pressure at mean sea level in January.*

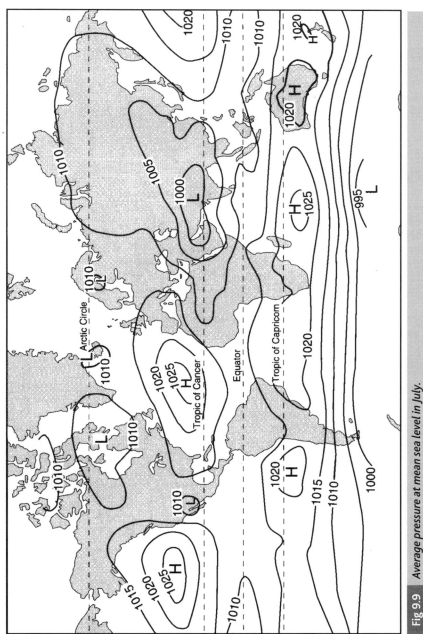

**Fig 9.9** Average pressure at mean sea level in July.

however, that in the South Atlantic the SE Trades blow right up to and across the equator throughout the whole year.

## Winds of the temperate zones

Westerly winds predominate on the poleward sides of the oceanic highs, but the winds of the temperate zones are subject to considerable variation in direction and force, because they are in the very disturbed region of travelling depressions and anticyclones which generally travel from west to east. In the southern hemisphere the westerlies blow right round the world with great consistency and frequently attain gale force which gives them the name of Roaring Forties.

## The Intertropical Convergence Zone (ITCZ)

This band of convergence is due to the meeting of air from the northern and southern hemispheres. This fluctuates seasonally, its range of movement being small in some areas of the ocean and very large in monsoon areas. The belt of separation between the NE and SE Trades has its maximum width on the eastern sides of the Atlantic and Pacific Oceans, and these regions of light and variable winds and calms are known as the doldrums. They are further characterised by very heavy convectional rain and thunderstorms. These stormy areas are easily identified on satellite images. The doldrums of the North Atlantic remain north of the equator throughout all seasons. Towards the western sides of the oceans the Trade winds tend to flow nearly parallel to one another and finally become easterly in direction.

## Monsoons

Large land masses become heated in summer and, as explained earlier in the chapter, pressure becomes low over the land and high over the sea. The reverse takes place in winter. The resulting wind circulations tend to persist throughout their particular seasons and are called **monsoons**. The most developed monsoons occur over southern and eastern Asia. They occur to a lesser degree in West Africa, America and Australia. In general, the monsoons of summer, being heavily moisture-laden from a long sea passage, are associated with much convection or orographic rain on reaching the coast. A winter monsoon is cool and dry with mainly fine weather, unless it has a long path over the sea.

### Monsoons of the Indian Ocean and China Sea

In northern summer the wind circulates anticlockwise round an extensive low centred over North West India. The pressure gradient extends beyond the North Indian Ocean into the southern hemisphere, so that the SE Trades of the South Indian Ocean cross the equator and, due to the rotational effect of the Earth, veer to SW as they are drawn into the monsoonal circulation. In the North Indian Ocean and western part of the North Pacific the Trade winds disappear completely during the period of the south-west monsoon. (See Figure 9.11.)

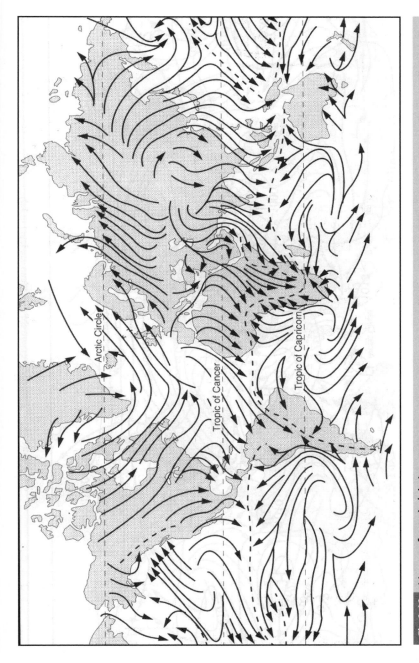

**Fig 9.10** Mean surface winds in January.

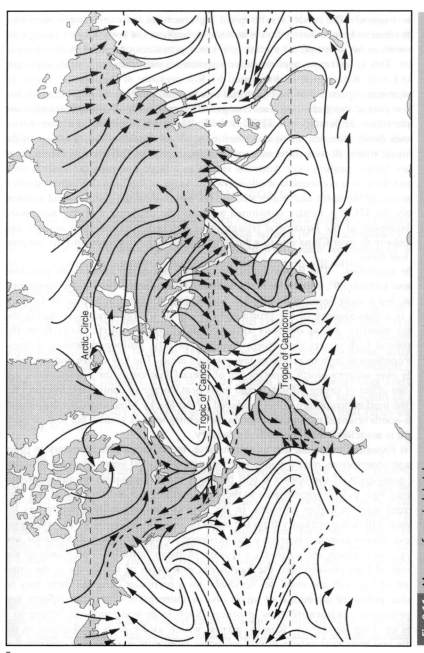

Arctic Circle

Tropic of Cancer

Tropic of Capricorn

**Fig 9.11** Mean surface winds in July.

The south-west monsoon season is from June to September (inclusive). In the Indian Ocean it blows as a strong wind reaching gale force at times. During its long passage over the warm sea it picks up a vast quantity of moisture and gives very heavy orographic rain on the windward coasts of India. Tropical cyclones occur in the Indian Ocean and Bay of Bengal, especially at the beginning and end of the south-west monsoon.

In the China Sea this summer monsoon is less strong than in the Indian Ocean and the rainfall is comparatively slight. More often than not it flows between south and east rather than south-west. Typhoons occur frequently, particularly in October.

In northern winter a large anticyclone is situated over Siberia and the north-east monsoon, which blows from October to March (with much less force than the summer monsoon), extends over the North Indian Ocean and China Sea, crosses the equator gradually backing to the NW and reaches Australia as the 'north-west monsoon'. In the North Indian Ocean this monsoon is dry and usually brings fine and clear weather. Along the coast of China and Indo-China the pressure gradient is steep and the winds stronger. Between January and April, in the China Sea and along the South China coast, periods of overcast drizzly weather with mist or fog occur. From February to April such periods may persist for over a week. The local name for these periods is Crachin. (See Figure 9.10 and Glossary.)

## Examples of other monsoons

When reading the following refer to Figures 9.8 and 9.9, which show world pressure distribution for January and July, respectively:

**Northern Australia and Indonesia.** Winds are south-easterly in winter and north-westerly in summer.

**West coast of Africa – Gulf of Guinea.** A south-west monsoon blows from June to September. The effect extends from latitude about 8°N to about 20°S.

**South-eastern part of the USA** (north of the Gulf of Mexico). The prevailing winds are north-westerly in winter and south-westerly in summer. They are disturbed by travelling depressions.

**East coast of Brazil** A north-east monsoon blows from September to March, when pressure over Brazil is low.

## Land and sea breezes

The principal wind systems of the world undergo local modifications for various reasons but due mainly to the unequal heating and cooling of land and sea. Land and sea breezes (a diurnal effect) occur most frequently and are more pronounced in countries where solar heating is powerful. They are experienced in temperate latitudes during warm summer weather but rarely exceed Force 3 and may extend 10 to 15 miles on either side of the coastline. In the tropics they sometimes reach Force 5 and may be felt 20 miles from the coast.

The most favourable conditions for land and sea breezes are anticyclonic, that is with clear skies and very light winds. Under such conditions in summer months the land heats up rapidly during the day whilst the sea remains cool. The warm air over the land rises and is replaced by air flowing in from over the sea. This sea breeze generally becomes appreciable after midday but in very warm weather may commence earlier if conditions are otherwise favourable. At night the process is reversed; the temperature of the sea does not change appreciably, whereas the land cools rapidly under clear skies after the sun goes down. The air, cooled by contact with the cold land, becomes denser and heavier and gravitates down the slope of the land towards the sea. The air over the sea is displaced by the land breeze and forced upwards. Higher up it flows back to the land, thereby completing the circulation. The land breeze is much weaker than the sea breeze, but its effect can be frustrating to small craft when trying to make port under sail. In tropical areas the land and sea breeze effect is almost routine.

Being local and temporary, land and sea breezes do not adjust themselves to the general pressure gradient. If the existing pressure gradient is steep and unfavourable it will completely mask the land and sea breezes. Conversely the wind force along the coast may be considerably increased when the gradient is favourable .

(See Anabatic and Katabatic winds in the Glossary.)

## Local winds

The following list gives the names and localities of the well known 'local winds'. A brief description of each is given in the Glossary.

**Bise**  Southern France

**Bora**  Eastern Adriatic

**Crachin**  China Sea

**Etesians**  Aegean Sea

**Föhn**  Swiss Alps. The same effect occurs in most parts of the world

**Haar**  Eastern Scotland and eastern parts of England

**Harmattan**  North-west Africa

**Kaus**  Persian Gulf

**Khamsin**  Egypt and North African coast

**Kharif**  Gulf of Aden

**Leste**  Madeira and North Africa

**Levanter**  Strait of Gibraltar

**Leveche**  South-east coast of Spain

**Libeccio**  Northern Corsica

**Maestro**  Adriatic Sea

**Marin**  Gulf of Lyons

**Mistral**  North-west coast of Mediterranean

**Norther**  Gulf of Mexico

**Pampero**  Rio de la Plata area

**Scirocco**  Mediterranean

**Shamal**  Persian Gulf and Gulf of Oman

**Solano**  Strait of Gibraltar

**Southerly buster**  South and South-east coast of Australia

**Sumatras**  Malacca Strait

**Tramontana**  West coast of Italy and Corsica.

**Vendavales**  East coast of Spain and Gibraltar Strait

## QUESTIONS

1 What is the relationship between wind direction and isobars at
   (a) Surface level and
   (b) In the free atmosphere?

2 (a) Account for the diurnal variation of surface wind speed over land areas.
   (b) Why is it negligible over the sea?

3 Define:
   (a) The geostrophic wind.
   (b) The gradient wind.

4 Describe and explain, with the aid of a simple diagram, the effect on the atmospheric pressure and wind circulation caused by widely different surface temperatures in adjacent regions:
   (a  At the surface.
   (b) At upper levels.
   (c) Give two notable examples.

5 Write notes on the following:
   (a) Trade winds.
   (b) Winds of the temperate zones.

6 Describe the characteristic weather of the doldrums.

7 In which regions of the Atlantic and Pacific oceans are the doldrums located?

8 Land and sea breezes:
   (a) Explain how they are caused.
   (b) In which middle-latitude season are they most frequent? Explain why.
   (c) What type of pressure system is most favourable for their development? Why?
   (d How might a sea breeze modify the direction and/or speed of the wind resulting only from the general pressure gradient, on a hot day in summer?

9 Explain fully how monsoons are caused and describe their general characteristics:
   (a) In summer.
   (b) In winter.

10 What are the months of the south-west and north-east monsoon seasons in the Indian Ocean?

11 Describe the weather conditions in the China Sea during the period of
   (a) The SW monsoon and
   (b) The NE monsoon.

# 10 SEA AND SWELL WAVES

## Introduction

Whenever the wind blows over the surface of the water the friction or tractive force of the wind creates waves in the water. Up to a limit, the stronger the wind, the higher will be the waves. In the open ocean the size of the waves depends also upon the depth of the water, the length of time the wind has been blowing and the 'fetch' which is the distance to windward of the observer over which the wind has blown. All this happens to be rather a convenient arrangement for the mariner because, as described later in this chapter, it enables him to estimate the force of the wind without the aid of instruments.

## Sea waves and swell

Waves caused directly by the wind blowing at the time of observation are known as **sea waves**. By contrast, **swell waves** will have been created some time beforehand by winds blowing in an area some considerable distance away. In the vicinity of the observer both the current wind and sea surface may be calm but there may be experienced a distinct wave motion, often with a long wave length in proportion to its height. These waves are known as swell waves, or simply swell. They often have an oily appearance and may have originated thousands of miles away.

## Characteristics of waves

The overall characteristics of sea waves are quite complex but the simple wave is described in these terms:

- ❖ **Length L** the horizontal distance in metres between successive crests or troughs.
- ❖ **Period T** the time in seconds between two successive crests or troughs past a fixed point.
- ❖ **Speed C** the rate in knots at which an individual crest advances.
- ❖ **Height H** is the vertical distance in metres from crest to trough.

For any individual wave it can be shown that:

Length L in metres = 1.56 x Period $T^2$
Speed C in knots = 3.1 x Period T

For example, given a period of 10 seconds, the length of wave will be 156 metres and its speed will be 31.0 knots.

The steepness of a wave is described by the ratio of Height to Length (H/L). The height is not specifically related to the other factors because when the steepness exceeds about 1 in 13 the wave will break.

## Wave trochoids

Although each wave has a forward motion, each particle of water at a wave's surface moves in a circular orbit of which the diameter is equal to a wave height (see Figures 10.1 (a) and (b)). The result is that at the crest the motion of each particle is forward and at the trough it is backward relative to the wave's motion. Below the surface the water particles take up similar orbits diminishing in size with the depth until, at a depth equal to the wave length, there is practically no motion due to the waves. The shape of this wave is described as a trochoid. Quite simply, a trochoid is the pattern which would be traced out if some kind of marker were to be fastened to the spoke of a wheel; if the wheel was then rolled along a flat surface next to a wall, a pattern as illustrated in Fig 10.1 (a) would be produced.

This shows in elevation a cross-section through a simple wave. The numbered arrows indicate the motion of a particle of water, or cork floating on the surface, as the wave form progresses in the direction indicated. Figure 10.1(b) shows that the cork describes a circle, but does not in fact move away from its mean position at the centre of the circle. The circular motion decreases rapidly with depth.

## Wave complications

In the open ocean, except perhaps in the case of a directional swell with no wind, the waves in any particular system are almost never uniform in their characteristics although their motion is always to leeward. When a wind starts to blow, trains of waves are created and move to leeward but, due to the wind turbulence and other factors, each wave train usually contains waves of differing length, period and height, the result being an irregular mixture in which only a few well-formed waves stand out. Another complication arises when sea waves and swell waves are present together, sometimes from the same direction, at other times from totally different directions. In such cases it may be difficult to distinguish sea from swell and synchronism may cause some of the waves to be very large.

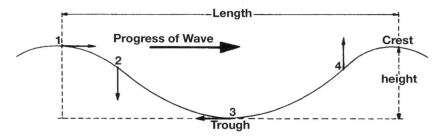

**Fig 10.1(a)**   *A simple wave form.*

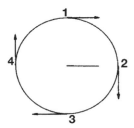

**Fig 10.1(b)**   *Resulting motion of a cork on the surface of the wave.*

## Wave groups

Wind-generated waves travel in groups, where large waves are continually overtaking smaller waves. This fact is important in handling a ship in heavy seas. The behaviour of a vessel depends to a great extent on her period of roll and pitch.

When the period of roll is less than the period of the wave the ship will tend to align her decks with the slope of the wave. A violent motion may result but little water will be shipped.

If the period of roll is greater than the period of the wave, the ship tends to dip her deck edge into the wave and to ship water whilst rolling more easily.

**A dangerous condition can arise with the waves abeam when the period of roll is the same as the period of the wave. Synchronisation may result in the ship being rolled over.**

In large merchant ships the period of roll is greatly in excess of the longest wave periods. On very small craft, however, with much shorter periods, synchronisation is a definite possibility. Since waves travel in groups, however, a series of individual waves all having the same period is an unlikely occurrence.

## Wave dimensions

A wave of a period of 2 seconds would have a length of about 6 metres and if the period were 10 seconds the length would be about 155 metres. These waves could be expected to have maximum heights of about 0.6 metres and 12 metres respectively. A long swell, however, with no wind present might have a period of 15 seconds and length of about 335 metres but a height of only 0.3 metres or so. The **maximum** wave height recorded to date is 25 metres.

The size of waves depends also on the duration of blow. Initially the waves are short and steep but if the wind continues to blow from the same direction they gradually become longer, and their heights increase. The high seas of the Roaring Forties for example are generated by fairly consistent strong winds of virtually unlimited fetch.

## Ocean waves in shoaling water

When an ocean wave comes into shallow water, beginning at a depth of half the wave length, its speed and length is reduced though its height stays the same, but the wave breaks when the depth is about $1^1/_2$ times its height. When approaching a beach at an oblique angle a wave tends to change its direction so that the advancing edge or front becomes parallel to the beach. It is important to remember that in relatively shallow and enclosed areas such as the North Sea and the Baltic, although the waves are unlikely to obtain oceanic dimensions, they are at times steep and short and therefore dangerous.

## Tsunami

These waves were also known as tidal waves, but they are not caused by the tides. Their cause is sudden, large-scale movement of the seabed such as the violent motion caused by earthquakes, volcanoes or landslides. The waves which are produced have small heights and long wavelengths in the deep ocean and travel very rapidly away from their source. Their speed of travel is related to the square root of the depth of the water so the tsunami begins to slow down as it reaches shallow coastal waters. As the front part of the wave slows the water begins to pile up, the height of the wave increases and the wave length decreases. The tsunami, which may pass unnoticed in deep water, can have disastrous effects in coastal areas due to the great quantity of energy that it carries.

The Pacific is prone to tsunamis because of the seismic activity which takes place there. Indeed the word tsunami is derived from Japanese and means harbour wave. A warning service has been set up to detect possible tsunami-producing events. Since December 2004, work has begun to instigate a similar service in the Indian Ocean. Tsunamis are extremely rare in the Atlantic but have been recorded, notably the tsunami which hit Lisbon in 1755.

Investigate http://www.tsunami.noaa.gov/ for a good description of tsunamis and their effects.

## Tidal streams

A tide flowing against the wind (weather tide) will often cause waves to heap up and break at the crest. A lee tide tends to flatten the sea.

Tidal races can be hazardous as the seas produced tend to be confused. Such areas are indicated on charts and in sailing directions. The waves in a race often arrive from several directions with little warning. The very strong currents experienced in some tidal races (eg the Portland Race and the Alderney Race) can make it very difficult to con low-powered craft.

## Freak waves

When swell and waves are moving in different directions, the crest of several waves may arrive simultaneously at one point. This can produce a wave of unusual height in an otherwise moderate sea. Troughs synchronising in a similar manner will produce what has been described as a 'hole in the ocean'.

Very steep and dangerous waves are sometimes experienced with south-westerly winds off the east coast of South Africa south of Durban, in the vicinity of the Aghulas Current and its inshore counter-current. Investigations are still continuing into the apparent complete disappearance of a number of ships, including large bulk carriers, which it is believed may be attributed to this cause.

### Practical value of wave data

Information about wave performance in the oceans is needed for the following purposes:

1 To assist in the preparation and issue of information of weather routeing for ships (see Chapter 24).

2 For research into the behaviour of ships in a seaway and into ship designs generally.

3 For the design and orientation of harbours and breakwaters and design of oil platforms at sea.

4 To assist in the forecast of wave conditions on exposed coasts (eg exposed anchorages).

5 For meteorological and oceanographical research generally.

## Observing the waves

In the deck log aboard a ship it is customary to record wave conditions descriptively, eg 'Slight Sea', 'Heavy Swell', etc. Similar phrases are customarily used in weather bulletins for shipping to describe actual and forecast waves. A more exact method of describing waves when coding weather reports for sending to meteorological services is to report their estimated height and period. Such observations are admittedly difficult to make with any accuracy from the high bridge of a fast-moving ship, but instructions are given to the observers by Port Meteorological Officers and some proficiency can be attained with practice. The synoptic maps, broadcast to shipping by facsimile, concerning actual and forecast wave conditions, give height in metres but rarely include period.

The following tables giving descriptions and approximate equivalent heights of sea and swell waves have been agreed by the WMO for international use. *(These tables are not used for coded weather reports and are only intended for guidance.)*

| SEA WAVES | | |
|---|---|---|
| **Description** | **Height** | |
| | *Metres* | *Feet* |
| 0  Calm (glassy) | 0 | 0 |
| 1  Calm (rippled) | 0–0.1 | 0–0.33 |
| 2  Smooth (wavelets) | 0.1–0.5 | 0.33–1.66 |
| 3  Slight | 0.5–1.25 | 1.66–4 |
| 4  Moderate | 1.25–2.5 | 4–8 |
| 5  Rough | 2.5–4 | 8–13 |
| 6  Very rough | 4–6 | 13–20 |
| 7  High | 6–9 | 20–30 |
| 8  Very high | 9–14 | 30–45 |
| 9  Phenomenal | Over 14 | Over 45 |

| SWELL WAVES | | | |
|---|---|---|---|
| Description | Approximate height | | |
| | | Metres | Feet |
| 0 No swell | | 0 | 0 |
| 1 Short or medium<br>2 Long | } Weak | Less than 2 | Less than 6 |
| 3 Short<br>4 Medium<br>5 Long | } Moderate | 2–4 | 6–12 |
| 6 Short<br>7 Medium<br>8 Long | } High | Greater than 4 | Greater than 12 |

## The Beaufort scale

This was first produced by Admiral Beaufort in 1808, subsequently he was a distinguished and long-serving hydrographer of the Navy. The scale provides a practical means of estimating the force of the wind from the appearance of the sea. Originally the categories were related to characteristics of manoeuvring various categories of sailing ships of the period eg 'Force 6 – That in which a well-conditioned man-of-war could just carry single-reefed topsails and topgallant sails'. Although these criteria no longer appear, the 'Sea Criterion' as defined by Beaufort for the same wind strength – 'Large waves begin to form; the white foam crests are more extensive everywhere. Probably some spray – are unaltered.

Watchkeepers should thoroughly familiarise themselves with the scale. Wind speeds are stated for a height of 10 metres above sea level.

## State of sea photographs for estimating wind speeds

The colour photographs between pages 70 and 71 illustrate the appearance of the sea corresponding to the Beaufort wind scale. Their purpose is to assist observers in estimating the wind speed when making weather reports. The description of the sea is according to the **Sea Criterion** laid down by the World Meteorological Organisation.

The appearance of the sea may be affected also by **fetch** (see Glossary), depth of water, swell, heavy rain, tidal streams and the lag effect between the wind getting up and the sea increasing.

Probable wave heights and probable maximum wave heights have been added only as a rough guide to show what may be expected in sea areas remote from land. In enclosed waters, or when near land with an offshore wind, wave heights will be smaller and the waves steeper.

## BEAUFORT WIND SCALE

| Beaufort number | Mean velocity | | Descriptive term | Deep Sea Criterion | Probable height of waves in metres* |
|---|---|---|---|---|---|
| | knots | m/s | | | |
| 0 | Less than 1 | 0–0.2 | Calm | Sea like a mirror | |
| 1 | 1–3 | 0.3–1.5 | Light air | Ripples with the appearance of scales are formed but without foam crests. | 0.1 (0.1) |
| 2 | 4–6 | 1.6–3.3 | Light breeze | Small wavelets, still short but more pronounced. Crests have a glassy appearance. | 0.2 (0.3) |
| 3 | 7–10 | 3.4–5.4 | Gentle breeze | Large wavelets. Crests begin to break. Foam of glassy appearance. Perhaps scattered white horses. | 0.6 (1) |
| 4 | 11–16 | 5.5–7.9 | Mod breeze | Small waves, becoming longer: fairly frequent white horses | 1 (1.5) |
| 5 | 17–21 | 8.0–10.7 | Fresh breeze | Moderate waves, taking a more pronounced long form; many white horses are formed. (Chance of some spray.) | 2 (2.5) |
| 6 | 22–27 | 10.8–13.8 | Strong breeze | Large waves begin to form, the white foam crests are more extensive everywhere. (Probably some spray.) | 3 (4) |
| 7 | 28–33 | 13.9–17.1 | Near gale | Sea heaps up and white foam from breaking waves begins to be blown in streaks along the direction of the wind. | 4 (5.5) |
| 8 | 34–40 | 17.2–20.7 | Gale | Moderately high waves of greater length; edges of crests begin to break into spindrift. The foam is blown in well-marked streaks along the direction of the wind. | 5.5 (7.5) |
| 9 | 41–47 | 20.8–24.4 | Strong gale | High waves. Dense streaks of foam along the direction of the wind. Crests of waves begin to topple, tumble and roll over. Spray may affect visibility. | 7 (10) |
| 10 | 48–55 | 24.5–28.4 | Storm | Very high waves with long overhanging crests. the resulting foam in great patches is blown in dense white streaks along the direction of the wind. On the whole the surface of the sea takes a white appearance. The tumbling of the sea becomes heavy and shocklike. Visibility affected. | 9 (12.5) |
| 11 | 56–63 | 28.5–32.6 | Violent storm | Exceptionally high waves. (Small and medium-sized ships might be for a time lost to view behind the waves.) The sea is completely covered with long white patches of foam lying along the direction of the wind. Everywhere the edges of the wave crests are blown into froth. Visibility affected. | 11.5 (16) |
| 12 | 64+ | 32.7+ | Hurri-cane | The air is filled with foam and spray. Sea completely white with driving spray; visibility very seriously affected. | 14 (–) |

*Notes*
(1) It must be realised that it will be difficult at night to estimate wind force by the Sea Criterion.
(2) The lag effect between increase of wind and increase of sea should be borne in mind.
(3) Fetch, depth, swell, heavy rain and tide effects should be considered when estimating the wind force from the appearance of the sea.

*This table is intended only as a guide to show roughly what may be expected in the open sea, remote from land. In enclosed waters, or when near land with an offshore wind, wave heights will be smaller, and the waves steeper. Figures in brackets indicate probable max height of waves.

WARNING: FOR A GIVEN WIND FORCE, SEA CONDITIONS CAN BE MORE DANGEROUS NEAR LAND THAN IN THE OPEN SEA, IN MANY TIDAL WATERS WAVE HEIGHTS ARE LIABLE TO INCREASE CONSIDERABLY IN A MATTER OF MINUTES.

Very few ships carry an anemometer, and this would only indicate the relative wind aboard a moving ship. What is needed is the true wind force and direction and the Beaufort scale provides the best method of making this important observation.

The line of sight at right angles to the wave's line of advance indicates the true direction of the wind.

Both these observations are relatively easy to make in daylight but difficult on a dark night, especially with light winds, particularly in a fast ship; care and experience and common sense are needed, using the feel of the wind on the face or wetted finger, first of all to determine the force and direction of the relative wind. If the ship's speed is (say) 15 knots and the relative wind is nil, there is a 15 knot wind from right aft. If the relative wind seems to be about 15 knots from abeam, then the true wind is on the quarter, about 20 knots (fresh breeze). This can be solved fairly simply from a vector triangle, one side being the ship's course and speed, another side the direction and speed of the relative wind, the third side will be the direction and speed of the true wind. (See Marine Observer's Handbook, supplied free by the Meteorological Office to all British Selected ships and containing a table for converting relative to true wind by inspection.)

Woods Hole Oceanographic Institute has an interesting website at http://www.whoi.edu/ which offers a great deal of information on oceanography.

## QUESTIONS

1 Define each of the following terms in relation to ocean waves: Length, Period, Height, Speed.

2 If the wave period (an average of several observations) was found to be 5.4 seconds, find its approximate speed and length. (Ans Speed C = 17 knots. Length L = 44 metres.)

3 Describe the effects of fetch, duration of blow, tidal streams and shoaling water on:
   (a) Sea waves.
   (b) Swell.

4 List some of the practical uses to which wave data is put by meteorological and other authorities ashore.

5 Ship handling in heavy seas:
   (a) Describe how different wave periods can affect a ship's behaviour.
   (b) What action can be taken to avoid or modify dangerous rolling?

# 11 AIR MASSES AND ASSOCIATED WEATHER

An air mass may be described as a huge body of homogeneous air covering thousands of square miles; throughout the air mass **temperature** and **humidity** are more or less **uniform** in any one horizontal plane. An air mass could be broadly classified, therefore, as warm or cold and moist or dry; the terms are relative. Classification of air masses is described later.

The lower levels of the atmosphere automatically assume the characteristics of the underlying surface. Thus an air mass originating over very cold land in winter would be cold and dry, whereas an airstream approaching the land after a long sea passage from warmer latitudes would be relatively warm and moist.

## Source regions

The area in which an air mass originates is called the source region. The principal source regions are the large anticyclonic areas which lie to the north and south of the disturbed westerlies, ie the polar highs covering the polar caps, the oceanic sub-tropical highs and the continental highs; the latter being the anticyclones which develop over large land masses during winter months. (See Figures 9.8 and 9.9 showing world pressure distribution for January and July respectively.) Other parts of the world may become source regions for short periods.

In all these areas the pressure gradient is generally slight and the horizontal movement of air is slow, thus allowing plenty of time for the surface characteristics (temperature and humidity) to penetrate upwards to considerable heights.

## General classification of air masses

This is broadly based on the source regions, and the terms used to describe a particular type of air mass may seem a little confusing at first. For example, so-called **Polar air** does not originate from the polar caps but from subpolar regions. Air coming from polar regions is called **Arctic air** or **Antarctic air**, as appropriate. Similarly so called **Tropical air** does not flow from tropical latitudes but from the sub-tropical belts. An airstream flowing from between the Trade wind belts is classified as **equatorial air**. These main types are sub-classified as **maritime** or **continental**; the former originating over the sea and being moist in character, the latter flowing from dry land and generally fairly dry, but it is important to remember that the history of an air mass can change its characteristics.

The table of Air Mass Classification given below is general. Almost any area of the world can occasionally act as a source region.

### Characteristics of an air mass

The characteristics of an air mass are governed by three factors:

1 The ORIGIN which determines temperature and humidity.

2 The PATH which determines the modifications which take place at the surface. As an air mass moves away from its source region it assumes the characteristics of the surface over which it is passing; thus warm dry air moving over a cold sea will pick up moisture and gradually become cooler in the layers near the surface.

3 The AGE of an air mass determines the height to which the surface characteristics will penetrate.

Modifications to the surface temperature may alter the stability of the air mass.

| CLASSIFICATION OF AIR MASSES | | |
|---|---|---|
| Type | Abbreviation | Origin |
| Arctic maritime air | Am or mA | Over seas in Arctic or Antarctic regions |
| Arctic continental air | Ac or cA | Over land in Arctic or Antarctic regions |
| Polar maritime air | Pm or mP | Over seas in sub-polar regions |
| Polar continental air | Pc or cP | Over land in sub-polar regions |
| Tropical maritime air | Tm or mT | Over seas in the sub-tropics |
| Tropical continental air | Tc or cT | Over land in the sub-tropics |
| Equatorial air | E | Very low latitudes between the Trade wind belts |

## Air mass weather

**Air mass characteristics are based on the following general principles:**

### Cold air moving over a warm surface

**1** Becomes heated at the surface by contact.

**2** The warmed air rises, not bodily but in vertical columns (called convection currents), through the colder environment. The height to which convection currents will go depends on a number of factors which are explained in Chapter 4.

**3** The greater the temperature difference between the air mass and the underlying surface the more vigorous will be the convection currents.

**4** If the rising air goes high enough and there is sufficient moisture present, cumuliform cloud will appear and, with further development, there may be some precipitation, characteristically in the form of isolated showers. (See Figure 11.1.)

**5** This is called unstable air because vertical movement is stimulated, especially when the air is humid.

**6** An unstable air mass is favourable for good visibility, except in showers.

### Warm air moving over a cold surface

**1** Becomes cooled at the surface by contact.

**2** Surface friction causes turbulent mixing of the air at and near the surface. This diffuses the cooling upwards from a few feet to a height of 500 metres

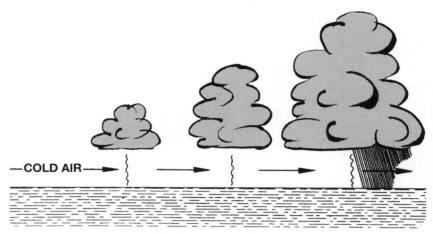

**WARM SEA SURFACE**

Fig 11.1

**FORCE 0 (CALM)** Wind speed less than 1 knot

Sea like a mirror. *Photo by N C Horner*

**FORCE 1 (LIGHT AIR)** Wind speed 1–3 knots: mean, 2 knots

Ripples with the appearance of scales are formed, but without foam crests. *Photo by G J Simpson*

**FORCE 2 (LIGHT BREEZE)**   Wind speed 4–6 knots: mean, 5 knots

Small wavelets, still short but more pronounced – crests have a glassy appearance and do not break. *Photo by G Bartlett*

**FORCE 3 (GENTLE BREEZE)**   Wind speed 7–10 knots: mean, 9 knots

Large wavelets. Crests begin to break. Foam of glassy appearance. There is the possibility of scattered white horses. *Photo by G Bartlett*

**FORCE 4 (MODERATE BREEZE)** Wind speed 11–16 knots: mean, 13 knots

Small waves, becoming longer; fairly frequent white horses. *Photo by I G MacNeil*

**FORCE 5 (FRESH BREEZE)** Wind speed 17–21 knots: mean, 19 knots

Moderate waves, taking a more pronounced long form; many white horses are formed. There is the chance of some spray. *Photo by J F P Galvin*

**FORCE 6 (STRONG BREEZE)**   Wind speed 22–27 knots: mean, 24 knots

Large waves begin to form; the white foam crests are more extensive everywhere. There is probably some spray. *Photo by D Ogle*

**FORCE 7 (NEAR GALE)**   Wind speed 28–33 knots: mean, 30 knots

Sea heaps up and white foam from breaking wave blown in streaks along the direction of the wind. *Photo by G J Simpson*

**FORCE 8 (GALE)** Wind speed 34–40 knots: mean, 37 knots

Moderately high waves of greater length; edges of crests begin to break into spindrift. The foam is blown in well marked streaks along the direction of the wind. *Photo by W A E Smith*

**FORCE 9 (STRONG GALE)** Wind speed 41–47 knots: mean, 44 knots

High waves. Dense streaks of foam along the direction of the wind. Crests of waves begin to topple, tumble and roll over. Spray may affect visibility. *Photo by: J P Laycock*

**FORCE 10 (STORM)**   Wind speed 48–55 knots: mean, 52 knots

Very high waves with long overhanging crests. The resulting foam, in great patches, is blown in dense white streaks along the direction of the wind. On the whole, the surface of the sea takes a white appearance. The tumbling of the sea becomes heavy and shock-like. Visibility is affected. *Photo by J P Laycock*

## FORCE 11 (VIOLENT STORM)   Wind speed 56-63 knots: mean, 60 knots

Exceptionally high waves. (Small and medium-sized ships might be for a time lost to view behind the waves.) The sea is completely covered with long white patches of foam lying along the direction of the wind. Everywhere the edges of the wave crests are blown into froth. Visibility is affected. *Photo © Crown*

**FORCE 12 (HURRICANE)**   Wind speed greater than 63 knots

The air is filled with foam and spray. The sea is completely white with driving spray; visibility is very seriously affected. *Photo by J F Thomson*

(1,500 feet) or more depending on the speed of the wind and the roughness of the surface.

3   This colder, denser, heavier air forms a shallow layer on the surface and is said to be stable because it offers resistance to any vertical displacement. (See Chapter 4.)

4   If the air contains enough moisture a layer of cloud will form below the top of the turbulence layer. (See Figure 11.2.) If the air is dry or fairly dry, skies are likely to be clearer.

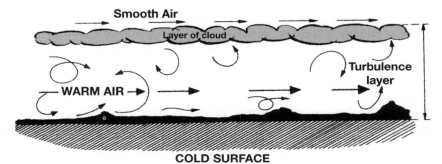

**Smooth Air**

Layer of cloud

**Turbulence layer**

**WARM AIR**

**COLD SURFACE**

Fig 11.2

5   Fog can form in light winds if the temperature of the surface is below the dew point temperature of the air. Types of fog and their causes are discussed in Chapter 8.

6   Poor visibility is favoured by a stable air mass.

## Details of specific air mass types

Figures 11.3 and 11.4 illustrate paths taken by some typical types of air masses. They should be studied in conjunction with the following descriptions of weather generally associated with each type. Bear in mind that the air mass characteristics described apply equally to both northern and southern hemispheres.

### Polar maritime (Pm) air

Cold air from higher latitudes moving over a relatively warm surface. Cool, unstable, cumuliform cloud, possibly with isolated squally showers (particularly when the air is moving quickly across the isotherms), very good or excellent visibility except in showers. For example, a north-westerly airstream reaching the British Isles after a long sea passage. This same airstream, when passing over cold land in winter, may become stable with low stratus cloud or fog.

## Polar continental (Pc) air

In winter this is a very cold stable airstream with a low moisture content. Little change takes place during its passage over cold land. Clear skies can generally be expected but, when such an air mass moves over a relatively warm sea surface, evaporation and warming take place; this results in instability and cumuliform cloud, wintry showers may occur. It thus assumes the characteristics of polar maritime air. For example, in winter, polar continental air from North America becomes polar maritime air during its passage eastwards across the Atlantic Ocean.

In summer the polar continental air mass will remain dry and cloudless as it moves over land which is warmer than at the source but, when subjected to surface heating over long distances, it becomes converted into a warm air mass which, if it then moves over a cool sea, becomes stable, picks up moisture, and fog or low stratiform cloud may form.

## Arctic maritime (Am) air

Originates over ice and snow surfaces and is thus very cold at all levels. Because of its low temperature the moisture content is low, but moisture is picked up over the sea as warming takes place from below. The weather then becomes similar to that of polar maritime air but much colder and more intense in character, because the difference between air and sea temperatures is more marked than in polar maritime air. Cumulus or cumulonimbus clouds form and squally showers of rain or hail occur.

## Arctic continental (Ac) air*

This is similar in character to polar continental air.

## Tropical maritime (Tm) air

Warm and very moist air moving into higher latitudes passes over a sea surface which becomes progressively cooler. A stable air mass in which very widespread advection fog, or low stratiform cloud or drizzle may be encountered. Orographic rain at high coastlines is common. Example: Widespread advection fog often encountered over the relatively cool waters of the northeast Pacific and the Grand Banks of Newfoundland area in the North Atlantic.

In summer, when moving over hot land it may become very unstable giving cumulus cloud with showers and possibly thunderstorms.

## Tropical continental (Tc) air

Very warm and dry at source. Moving into higher latitudes it becomes cooled in the lower layers and remains dry whilst passing over land. When moving over

---

*Air masses which originate over the snow covered areas of the Arctic have similar characteristics to polar continental air and, for this reason, are designated as such in the North American continent.*

the sea its temperature is higher than that of the sea surface and, although some moisture is picked up, there is generally very little cloud or precipitation because convection is arrested at a low level in the stable air. An air mass originating in desert regions may carry quantities of fine dust for thousands of miles, thus hazy conditions are not uncommon in a tropical continental air mass. (See Figures 11.3 and 11.4.)

### Warm polar maritime (wPm) air or returning polar maritime (rPm) air

A polar maritime air mass, after moving into lower latitudes where it becomes warmed in the lower level, sometimes curves round and increases its latitude again. It then undergoes cooling in the surface layers, becomes stable and assumes the characteristics of tropical maritime air. On such occasions it is called **returning polar maritime air** or **warm polar maritime air** (See Figures 11.3 and 11.4.)

### Equatorial (E) air masses

Warm, moist and often very unstable, especially after surface heating over land when convection currents carry large quantities of moisture to high levels forming cumulus and cumulonimbus cloud and producing copious rainfall.

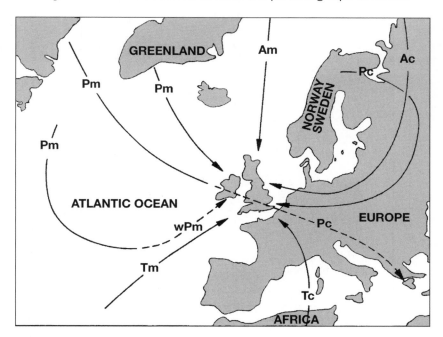

**Fig 11.3** *Air masses reaching the British Isles.*

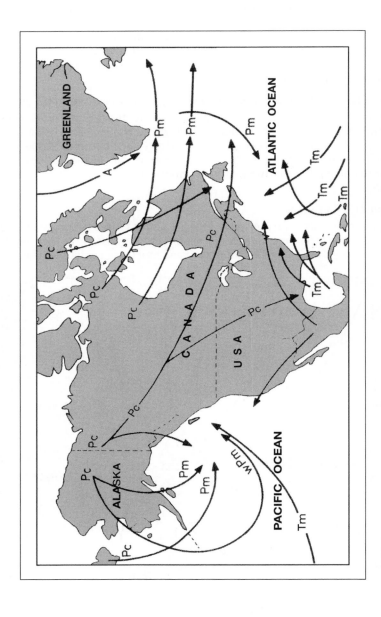

**Fig 11.4** Some paths of typical air masses of the N American continent and adjacent waters

## QUESTIONS

**1** Define the term air mass.

**2** In which parts of the world are the principal source regions of air masses found?

**3** Describe the characteristics of the following air mass types, at source only: Pm, Pc, Am, Ac, Tm, Tc, E.

**4** Describe the weather generally associated with a Tm air mass in temperate latitudes when moving over:
(a) The sea and increasing latitude.
(b) Hot land in summer.
(c) Cold land in winter.

**5** Describe the typical characteristics of Pm air on moving to lower latitudes.

**6** Describe the path taken by a Pm air mass which approaches the British Isles from the Atlantic Ocean as a wPm air mass.

**7** Classify an air mass whose source region is Northern Canada in winter. Describe its initial characteristics and the changes you would expect as it moves eastwards across the Atlantic Ocean.

# 12 ISOBARIC PATTERNS

Out of seven characteristic isobaric patterns there are only two types of weather systems which are fundamental – the depression and the anticyclone – the remainder being either outward extensions from one of these or a neutral area between them.

These seven distinctive isobaric forms are:

❖ **Depression**
❖ **Anticyclone**
❖ **Secondary depression**
❖ **Trough**
❖ **Ridge or wedge**
❖ **Col**
❖ **Straight isobars**

Depressions, fronts and anticyclones are discussed in greater detail in later chapters.

## Depression (or low)

An area of low barometric pressure surrounded by an area in which the pressure is relatively high. The isobars are roughly circular or oval in shape and, in accordance with Buys Ballot's Law (see Chapter 9), the wind flows in an **anticlockwise** direction round the area of low pressure in the **northern hemisphere** (see Figure 12.1) and **clockwise** in the **southern hemisphere**.

It should be noted that in both hemispheres the surface wind flows slightly in towards the central area (see **Convergence** in Glosssary) where the worst weather is usually encountered.

Depressions are of greatly varying intensities and are usually associated with bad weather – ie much cloud and precipitation with strong or gale force winds,

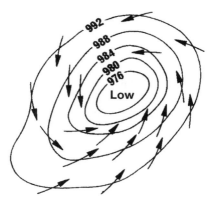

| **Fig 12.1** | *The Isobaric pattern of a depression* |

The wind circulation, anticlockwise in the northern hemisphere, is indicated by the arrows. In the southern hemisphere the wind flows clockwise round the low pressure centre. Note that the isobars are closer together near the centre.

especially near the centre of the system, the severity of the weather being governed mainly by the steepness of the pressure gradient and the moisture content of the surface air, but there are other important factors involved.

Despite the availability of official weather forecasts, it is important for a mariner to be able to recognise the precursory signs of bad weather and to know the weather sequence, shift of wind, etc which may be expected with the approach, passage and retreat of a well defined depression. Indeed, the safety of the ship may well depend on such knowledge and the ability to act on it.

The term **depression** is commonly applied to cyclones in latitudes which lie outside the tropics but may also be used to describe a weak tropical cyclone.

As a depression develops the pressure gradient becomes steeper and the winds stronger, isobars on each successive weather chart are drawn closer together and the depression is said to deepen. A weakening or dying depression is said to be filling up.

**Depressions tend to move towards areas of low or falling pressure and to steer round high pressure regions.**

## Anticyclone

A region of high pressure surrounded by an area of relatively low pressure. The isobars are roughly circular or oval in shape. In the northern hemisphere the wind circulates in a clockwise direction round the centre of high pressure; the converse is true for the southern hemisphere. (See Figure 12.2.)

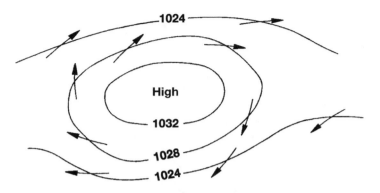

**Fig 12.2** *Anticyclone*

The wind circulation, clockwise in the northern hemisphere, is indicated by the arrows. Note that the isobars are more widely spaced near the centre of high pressure and that the surface wind tends to flow outwards from the centre.

### General characteristics

The pressure gradient is slight, winds are light near the centre. Weather is usually quiet, dry and settled. Land and sea breezes (see Chapter 9) are marked, especially during the warmest months of the year.

In summer the weather is generally dry, sunny and warm but within the outer portions of the system it is often cloudy with some rain.

In winter the weather may be one of two types:

(a) Cloudless sky with sharp frosts at night or radiation fog.
(b) The sky completely covered by stratus cloud. Dull, cold and foggy or misty weather may persist for some days. (See **Anticyclonic gloom** in Glossary.)

High pressure systems are usually slow moving by comparison with other systems and often remain stationary for long periods. An anticyclone is said to intensify as the pressure within the system rises, whereas when pressure falls, thereby weakening the system, it is said to decline.

## A secondary depression

A secondary depression is one which forms within the isobaric pattern of another (primary) depression. When the primary depression is old and filling up, the secondary may develop and deepen till it completely absorbs all traces of the primary. The secondary in Figure 12.3 has a steeper gradient and lower pressure at its centre than the primary or parent depression. **Note that secondary depressions often develop into much more vigorous systems than their primaries.**

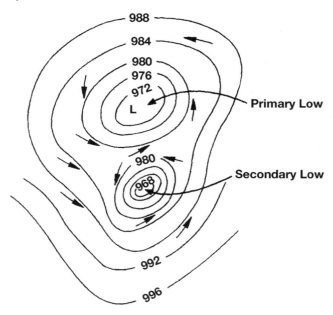

**Fig 12.3** *Primary and secondary depressions.*

## Trough of low pressure

This is distinguished on the weather chart by a system of isobars which appear sharply curved (concave towards low pressure) along a line called the trough line within a depression. (See Figure 12.6.)

A trough may be termed **deep** or **shallow** according to whether the curvature of the isobars is acute or gentle, respectively. The weather associated with a trough is generally cloudy with precipitation. (See **Line squall** in Glossary.)

### Fronts

Fronts, which are dealt with in later chapters, are all troughs; but a trough is not always a front. When the isobars of a depression or a tropical cyclone are circular the term trough refers to a line drawn through the centre of the system at right angles to the line of progression of the centre.

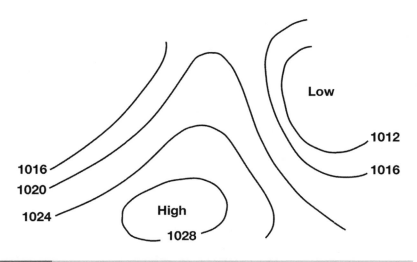

**Fig 12.4** *Ridge (or wedge) of high pressure.*

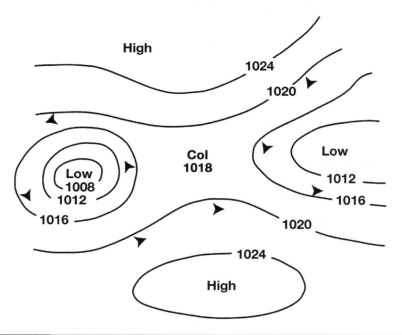

**Fig 12.5** *High, low and col.*

## Ridge (or wedge) of high pressure

A wedge-shaped extension of an anticyclone between two areas of low pressure. (See Figures 12.4 and 12.6.) The isobars assume their greatest curvature along the axis of the ridge. It is generally associated with the fair weather of the anticyclone, often having light winds along the central portion. A ridge in which the isobars are sharply curved generally moves faster than a 'flat' ridge.

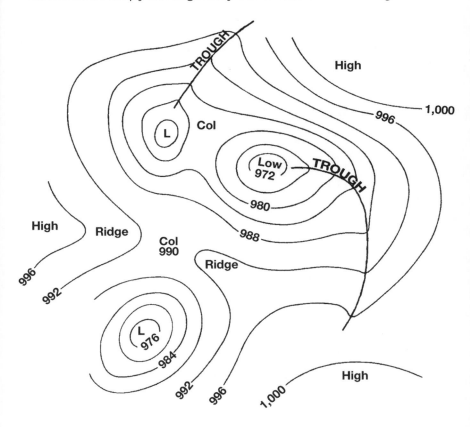

**Fig 12.6**   *Isobaric pattern illustrating high, low, trough, ridge and col.*

## Col

An area of indeterminate pressure located between two highs and two lows which are arranged alternately. (See Figures 12.5 and 12.6.) It is generally associated with light variable winds, often thundery in summer and dull or foggy or misty in winter. In Figure 12.5 the wind circulation round the four systems is shown by arrows. It is easy to see why the winds are variable within the col area.

## Straight isobars

An atmospheric pressure distribution in which the isobars run in more or less parallel straight lines across a large area. (See Figure 12.7.) It is usually the outlying portion of a large and distant depression or anticyclone.

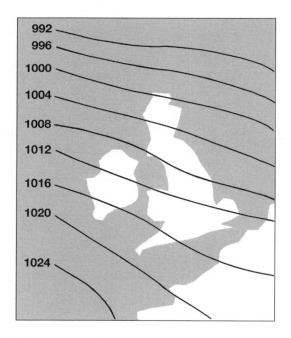

**Fig 12.7** *Straight isobars.*

## QUESTIONS

1  Name the seven characteristic isobaric forms.

2  Define the terms depression and anticyclone.

3  (a)  Sketch the isobars, fronts and wind circulation in a typical southern hemisphere depression.
   (b)  What are the two main factors which govern the severity of the weather in any middle-latitude depression?

4  In which direction do depressions tend to move?

5  Describe the general characteristics of an anticylcone:
   (a)  In summer.
   (b)  In winter.

6  Describe the weather associated with a col:
   (a)  In summer.
   (b)  In winter.

7  What mainly governs the weather conditions to be expected in a system of straight isobars?

# 13 FRONTS AND FRONTAL DEPRESSIONS

*Before proceeding with this chapter it is essential that the previous chapters have been read and understood.*

## Air mass boundaries

When two air masses of differing characteristics meet they do not mix freely but remain separated by a boundary called the frontal surface. Some mixing of the air masses does take place but only along this boundary which is really a narrow zone of transition often referred to as the mixing zone. Such a boundary is represented on the weather chart by a line called a *front*.

When two airstreams with different temperatures converge and meet, the warmer air tends to override the colder, denser, heavier air, whilst the colder air tends to undercut the lighter warm air. (See Figures 13.1 (a), (b) and (c).)

## The main frontal zones

The positions of frontal zones marking the boundaries between the principal air masses fluctuate constantly whilst their mean positions move north and south with the seasons.

See Figure 13.1 (d) and compare the mean positions of the frontal zones in January with those for July, but bear in mind that the day-to-day positions of these zones can vary considerably from those shown in the figure, especially in the temperate latitudes.

### The Arctic front

The Arctic front marks the transition between Arctic air and polar maritime air. There is a similar front in the North Pacific.

### The polar front

The polar front marks the boundary between polar and tropical air masses in the Atlantic and Pacific Oceans. In the North Atlantic its mean position in summer is from Newfoundland to Scotland. In winter it moves southwards and extends from Florida to south-west England.

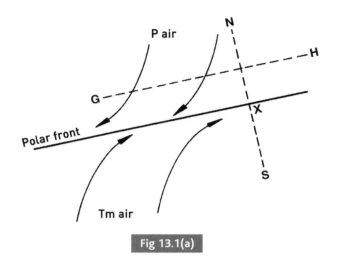

Fig 13.1(a)

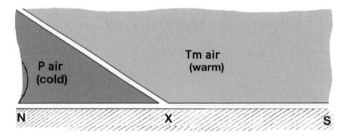

Fig 13.1(b)   *Vertical section across polar front.*

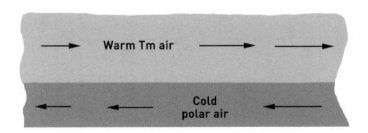

Fig 13.1(c)   *Vertical section along GH.*

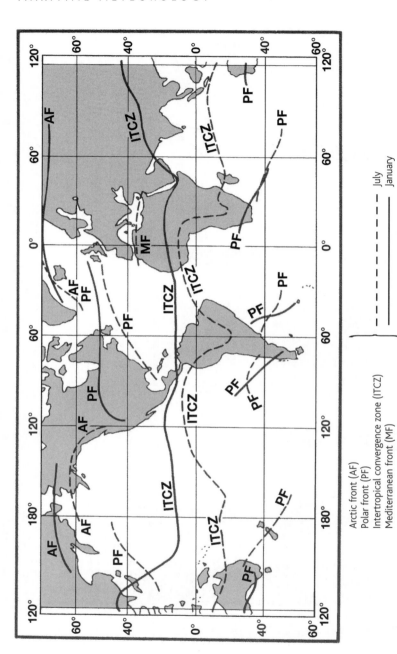

Arctic front (AF)
Polar front (PF)
Intertropical convergence zone (ITCZ)
Mediterranean front (MF)

— — — July
—— January

**Fig 13.1(d)** *Approximate mean positions of frontal zones.*

## The Mediterranean front

The Mediterranean front exists only in winter and extends from west to east across the Mediterranean, separating polar continental air originating from Europe and tropical continental air from North Africa.

## The intertropical convergence zone (ITCZ)

The intertropical convergence zone lies within the tropics and is a broad zone of separation between the NE and SE Trades which flow equatorwards from opposite hemispheres. It was formerly known as the *Intertropical Front* but this term has fallen into disuse, because the opposing air masses do not differ greatly in their characteristics and it bears little resemblance to other fronts.

The ITCZ crosses and recrosses the equator at several points and moves well north in the summer. Due to the very large land masses in the northern hemisphere the greater part of its length (in its mean position) lies north of the equator. Its range of movement is small over the oceans but may be very large over the continents. Areas of horizontal convergence along this belt vary from day to day in both position and activity but are generally associated with cloudy showery weather. (See Figure 13.1 (d).)

## *Frontal theory of formation of depressions*

Within the temperate zones cold air flowing from high latitudes encounters warm air moving from sub-tropical regions. The two air masses are separated by a frontal surface which slopes upward over the colder denser air at a gradient which varies from 1 in 40 to 1 in 200. (See Figures 13.1 (a), (b) and (c).)

The polar front tends to remain inactive so long as the warm and cold air masses flow parallel to one another but when they converge warm moist air is forced upwards over the cold frontal surface. This can result in the formation of much cloud and precipitation and often starts the mechanism which leads to the formation and development of a frontal depression. The sequence of events is described in the following paragraphs:

Under suitable conditions a small wave forms on the polar front, so that at this point there is a bulge of warm air protruding into the cold. See Figure 13.2 and note that the two air masses flow more or less parallel to one another along the polar front, except at the bulge where the winds are convergent. (See Convergence in Glossary.)

The wave continues to grow in size. Development usually follows and pressure falls at the crest of the wave.

Enlargement of the bulge continues and this is accompanied by a further fall in pressure. The isobars then assume the closed form of a depression and the wind circulates round the tip of the bulge. As pressure continues to fall the gradient becomes steeper and the winds stronger. (See Figure 13.3.)

Figure 13.3 shows the isobars and fronts of a well developed and active depression. The line LX is a warm front, since warm air is replacing cold air

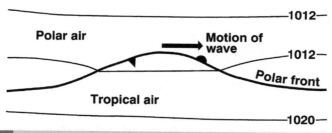

Fig 13.2 *Birth of a depression on polar front.*

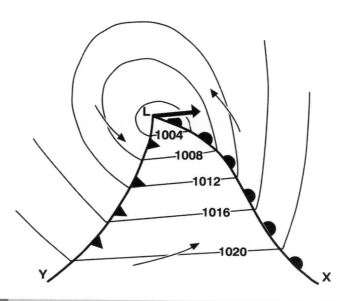

**Fig 13.3** *Early development.*

along this line. LY is a cold front since cold air is replacing warm air along this line. The warm and cold fronts are represented on the weather chart by the symbols shown in Figure 13.3. On working charts warm and cold fronts are represented by red and blue lines respectively.

The area between LX and LY is known as the 'warm sector' of the depression.

The centre of the depression will move along the polar front in a direction roughly parallel to the isobars in the warm sector and at a speed approximating to that of the air in the warm sector. (See Figure 13.3.)

## Clouds and weather at fronts

The tables showing weather sequence at warm and cold fronts should be studied in conjunction with figures 13.4 and 13.5, respectively. It is important to remember that the description of frontal weather which follows can only be general; every depression and every front is different, some fronts have no rain at all, others may have precipitation far in excess of the average. Similarly cloud structures do not always conform to the classic examples given.

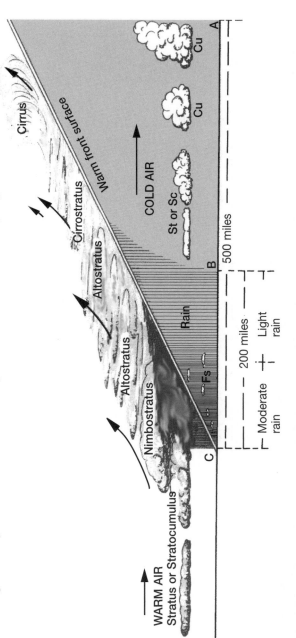

Fig 13.4  Vertical section across an average warm front.

| | Sequence of weather at a warm front | | |
|---|---|---|---|
| Element | On approaching | At passage | In warm sector |
| BAROMETER | Steady fall. | Stops falling. | Little change, sometimes unsteady in vigorous system. |
| WIND | Increasing; sometimes backing a little. † | Veers. ‡ | Steady in direction. |
| TEMPERATURE | Steady, or slow rise. | Rises. | Little change. |
| CLOUD | Ci, followed by Cs increasing, then As, then Ns with Fs below. | Low Ns and Fs. | St or Sc. |
| PRECIPITATION* | Light rain, soon becoming continuous and slowly increasing to moderate. | Rain stops or gives way to drizzle. | Intermittent slight rain, or drizzle, possibly fog; sometimes fair. |
| VISIBILITY | Good except in precipitation. | Poor, sometimes mist or fog. | Moderate or poor; sometimes widespread mist or fog. |

† Backing in northern hemisphere, veering in southern hemisphere.

‡ Veers in northern hemisphere, backs in southern hemisphere.

* If the air temperature is low enough snow will fall instead of rain.

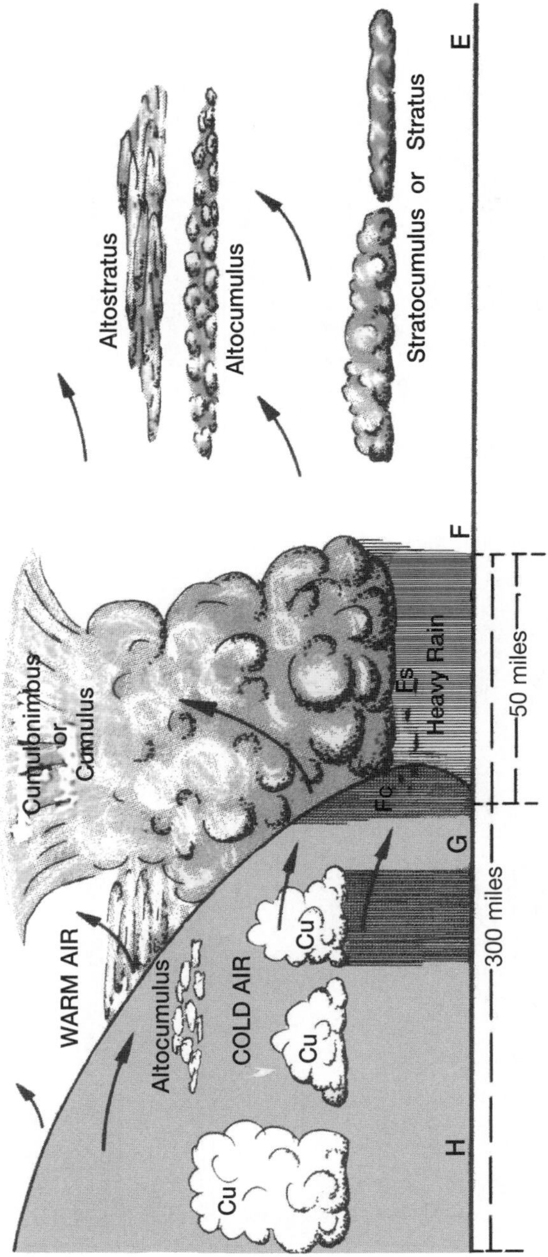

**Fig 13.5** Vertical section across an average cold front.

| | Sequence of weather at a cold front | | |
|---|---|---|---|
| Element | In warm sector | At passage | In the rear |
| BAROMETER | Little change at first; falls on near approach of front. | Shows sudden rise as front passes. | Continuous rise, rapid at first becoming slower. |
| WIND | Steady in direction, then backing † a little and becoming squally on near approach of front. | Sudden well-marked veer ‡ often with squall, sometimes followed by slight backing and strengthening. | Usually fairly steady in direction, except in squalls, decreases slowly. |
| TEMPERATURE | Little change, but marked fall with onset of frontal rain. | Sudden fall. | Little change, sometimes slow fall; varies in showers. |
| CLOUD | St or Sc, then Cu or Cb. | Cu or Cb with Fs and Fc below, sometimes very low Ns. | As, Ac, then Cu and possibly Cb with blue sky increasing. |
| PRECIPITATION * | Intermittent light rain or drizzle, sometimes fair. Heavy rain on near approach to front. | Heavy rain, sometimes hail perhaps thunder. | Heavy rain usually clears quickly and is followed by isolated showers becoming less frequent. |
| VISIBILITY | Moderate or poor, perhaps fog. | Reduced further in rain. | Rapid improvement as front passes, becomes very good except in showers. |

† *Backing in northern hemisphere, veering in southern hemisphere.*

‡ *Veering in northern hemisphere, backing in southern hemisphere.*

## The occluding of a depression

The cold front advances faster than the warm front and gradually overtakes it, commencing at the tip of the warm sector and working down the length of the front until the occluding process has been completed and all the tropical air has been lifted off the ground. Figures 13.6 and 13.7 show the stages in the occluding process. Note that the symbol for an occlusion is a combination of those used for warm and cold fronts. On working charts an occlusion is represented by a purple line.

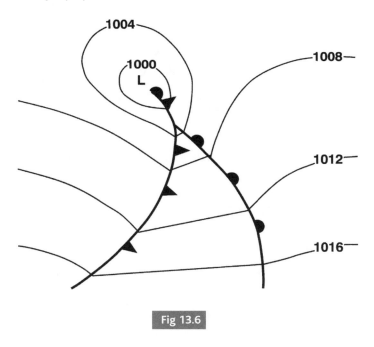

Fig 13.6

An occlusion is classified as warm or cold according to whether the overtaking polar air is warmer or colder than the retreating polar air, respectively. In the former case the overtaking air will override the colder air and, in the latter case, will undercut the warmer air. (See Figures 13.8 (a) and (b), 13.9(a) and (b).)

In Figures 13.8(a) and 13.9(a) the position of the upper front is indicated by a dotted line. Compare these two figures and notice that the line marking a cold occlusion is continuous with the line of the cold front whereas the warm occlusion is shown as a continuation of the warm front.

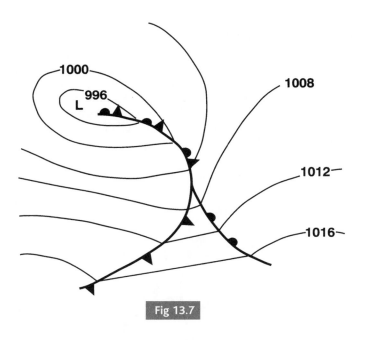

Fig 13.7

## Maturity and dissolution of a depression

The energy to develop and sustain an active frontal depression is derived mainly from the supply of air in the warm sector. Thus a depression having a wide warm sector will usually continue to deepen and grow in size whilst unoccluded, and often during the early stages of occlusion. Later, this development ceases and the speed and direction of movement of the centre is no longer related to that of the air in the warm sector, instead it becomes dependent on the general flow of air over a wide area. Movement tends to become slow at this stage and the depression may take several days to fill up, but the process of weakening is likely to be more rapid over a surface which is relatively cold.

The arrival of a new, more vigorous system can destroy the old circulation and cause it to fill up within 24 hours.

## Movement of depressions

❖ Small active depressions move faster than large dying ones.
❖ Small depressions tend to follow the flow of isobars in the general pattern, ie to follow the main stream.
❖ All depressions move from areas of rising pressure tendency towards areas of falling pressure tendency, ie from isallobaric high to isallobaric low. (See

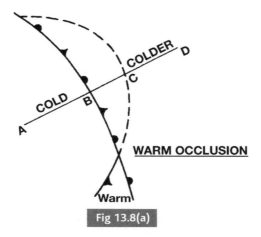

Fig 13.8(a)

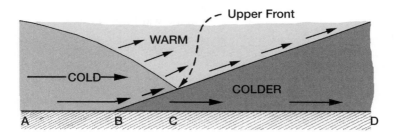

Fig 13.8(b)  Vertical section across warm occlusion.

**Pressure tendency** and **Isallobar** in Glossary.) If barometric tendencies are the same all round the centre of a depression it will remain stationary.

❖ Depressions tend to follow the flow of air round the perimeter of large, well established, warm anticyclones.

❖ An unoccluded depression moves in a direction parallel to the isobars in the warm sector and, at sea, at approximately the same speed as the surface wind in the warm sector.

❖ A partly occluded depression tends to slow down as the occluding process continues.

❖ A fully occluded depression becomes slow and sometimes erratic in movement, but generally moving in the direction of the average flow of air up to the tropopause. It also tends to move off to the left of its original track in the northern hemisphere and to the right in the southern hemisphere.

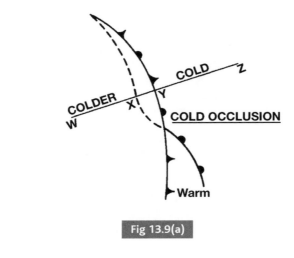

Fig 13.9(a)

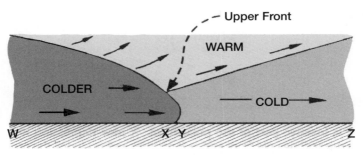

Fig 13.9(b)   *Vertical section across cold occlusion.*

❖ Large, completely occluded depressions are liable to become stationary, or nearly so, especially if there is little horizontal change in temperature within the area covered.

❖ A depression within a family (see Figure 13.10) follows the approximate path of its parent but tends to move 'off' towards lower latitudes.

❖ Secondary depressions tend to move with the main circulation of air round the primary.

❖ A non-frontal depression tends to move in the same direction as the strongest winds circulating round it.

## The future movement of a depression

This can be estimated by 'extrapolation'. That is, movement can be assumed to continue as shown by a succession of synoptic charts: but other factors should be taken into consideration, eg the bullet points above.

## A 'family' of depressions

The speed of movement of a cold front is greatest where the winds are strongest, that is, near the depression's centre. Near the perimeter of the system movement is less rapid and, as the whole system advances, the cold front tends to trail out well to the rear where it is continuous with the more or less inactive part of the polar front. A new depression may be formed on this trailing cold front and, as it matures and occludes, the process is repeated and another depression is born. In this way a family of three, four or five depressions may be formed, each new one on the trailing cold front of its parent. (See Figure 13.10.)

The cold air circulating in the rear of each system pushes the polar front further towards the sub-tropics; thus the track of each depression in the family commences in a lower latitude than that of its parent. Finally the cold air breaks through the polar front and flows equatorwards to feed the trade winds. Meanwhile an anticyclone builds up in the polar air, a new family commences to form on its poleward side and the whole cycle may be repeated.

A family of depressions approaching the British Isles from the Atlantic will give a period of very unsettled weather. The high pressure ridges between the lows will generally give short-lived periods of fine weather.

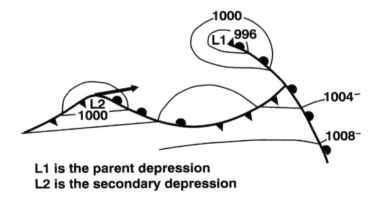

**L1 is the parent depression**
**L2 is the secondary depression**

Fig 13.10

## Formation of secondary depressions

A secondary depression is one which is contained within the circulation of a larger depression called the primary. The depression forming on the trailing cold front of a depression is an example of a secondary depression. (See Figure 13.10.)

Occasionally depressions can also form at the tip of the warm sector or on the warm front of a partly occluded depression. These secondaries form when the movement of the centre of the primary depression is blocked. (See Figure 13.11 (a) and (b).)

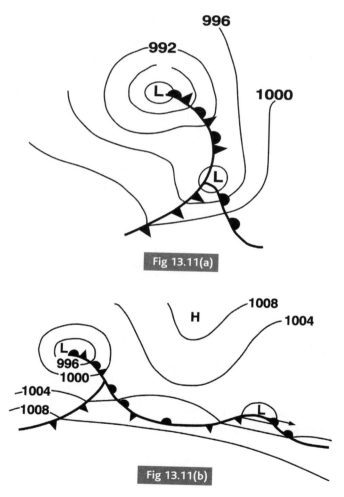

Fig 13.11(a)

Fig 13.11(b)

## Movement of secondary depressions

Secondaries have a tendency to move with the main flow of air round the primary centre. Their speed of movement is governed by the strength of wind in the primary circulation. As a secondary deepens it tends to approach the centre of the primary and eventually absorbs it completely. When, however, a secondary develops to about the same size and depth as the primary the two centres (which together form a 'dumb-bell' shaped depression) tend to rotate about one another – anticlockwise in the northern hemisphere. Secondaries which form at the occlusion point (Figure 13.11 (a)) move in the direction of the warm sector isobars and sometimes to the right of it.

## QUESTIONS

1 Name the three main frontal zones and the air masses they separate.

2 Describe the ITCZ and its associated weather.

3 Draw simple diagrams, in vertical cross-section, illustrating the warm and cold air masses at:
   (a) A warm front.
   (b) A cold front. Indicate the movement of each air mass with arrows.

4 Draw the international symbols used on synoptic weather charts for:
   (a) A warm front.
   (b) A cold front.
   (c) An occlusion. How would you know, from these symbols, in which direction the fronts are moving?

5 Describe, with the aid of sketches of isobars and fronts, the formation, growth and development (up to the early stage of occlusion) of a typical polar front depression.

6 Tabulate the sequence of cloud, wind, weather and instrumental readings you would expect to encounter whilst heading westwards through an unoccluded frontal depression in the N Atlantic. Assume you will pass to the south of the centre, through the warm and cold fronts.

7 Show, by means of simple sketches in vertical cross-section, the positions of the warm and cold air masses at:
   (a) A cold occlusion.
   (b) A warm occlusion.

8 Describe how the movement of a depression is related to barometric tendencies.

9 Sketch isobars and fronts in a 'family' of depressions (northern hemisphere). Describe briefly its formation and life history.

10 Describe the formation, development and movement of secondary depressions.

# 14 NON-FRONTAL DEPRESSIONS

*Look up Convergence and Divergence in the Glossary.*

Frontal depressions occur most frequently in temperate latitudes. It should not be assumed, however, that all depressions are associated with fronts.

## Formation of non-frontal depressions

(See Figure 14.1.)

1 Divergence at upper level reduces the total weight of air within a limited area and barometric pressure falls at the surface.
2 Surface air flows in towards the area of low pressure with cyclonic circulation.
3 Convergence at surface level causes ascent of moist air with consequent increase in cloud and precipitation.
4 For this system to remain active the outflow of air at upper level must exceed the inflow at the surface.
5 When the inflow of air at the surface exceeds the outflow at height the depression will fill up.

## Thermal depressions

Land surfaces heat up rapidly in the sun's rays, whereas the sea surface will change its temperature very little in the same period of time. Thus in some areas the distribution of land and sea surfaces results in unequal heating of the atmosphere in the surface layers.

Thermal depressions are often caused by strong surface heating over islands and peninsulas in summer, or over inland seas and lakes during winter when the land is very cold relative to the water surface. A slack pressure gradient gives very little wind and is therefore also favourable for the formation of thermal lows. Take the case of an island in the sun on a day when there is very little wind, the general mechanics of formation are as follows:

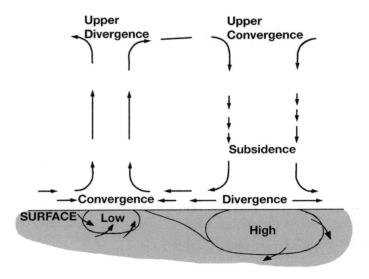

**Fig 14.1** *Formation of lows and highs.*

❖ Surface heating causes the air to expand vertically.
❖ This, in turn, gives high pressure at upper level. (Explanation in Chapter 9.)
❖ Divergence from the upper high causes reduction in the total weight of the air column and a fall in barometric pressure at the surface.
❖ Warm air over the island readily ascends to replace the outflow at higher level.
❖ Moist air from over the sea surface flows into the low pressure area and feeds the ascending air.
❖ The system is further stimulated by the process of condensation which releases latent heat above the level of the cloud base.

## Instability depressions (polar depressions)

Instability or polar depressions often form in the cold air to the rear of a depression. They are caused by surface heating where a cold polar airstream crosses the relatively warm ocean. The latent heat released when water vapour condenses to form the convection cloud produces an area of low pressure.

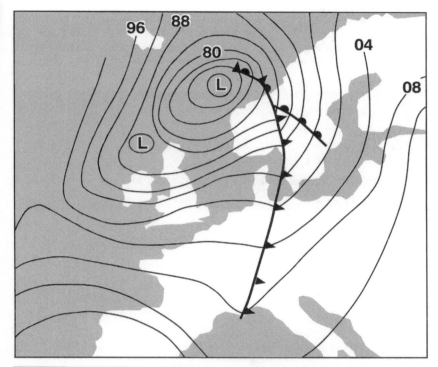

**Fig 14.2** *An instability (polar depression).*

Most thermal lows give heavy showers or thunderstorms rather than periods of continuous bad weather. Beware of sudden violent squalls with large wind shifts and often complete reversal in wind direction in the vicinity of thunderstorms.

## Orographic depressions (lee depressions)

An airstream which is obstructed by a mountain range may sweep around the ends of the range. Air, does however, tend to 'pile up' on the weather side, producing an increase in surface pressure. On the lee side an eddy effect tends to reduce pressure. Often this produces only a slight ridge of high pressure on the weather side and a slight trough of low pressure on the lee side, but a shallow depression can develop on the lee side. A depression which forms in this way can become very intense if conditions are favourable and may continue to deepen as it moves away. Later it may become very similar to a frontal depression. Orographic depressions tend to be associated with certain geographical locations. They often form to the east of the Rockies and are associated with the region near Genoa in northern Italy, when the wind blows southwards across the Alps.

## QUESTIONS

1  Describe the formation of:
   (a) A thermal depression.
   (b) An orographic depression.

2  Describe the formation and weather associated with an instability depression.

# 15 ANTICYCLONES

The horizontal motion of the air in an anticyclone has a major influence on its properties.

An area of convergence is one in which the horizontal inflow of air is greater than the horizontal outflow at the same level. An area of divergence is one in which the horizontal outflow exceeds the horizontal inflow. Both of these motions are accompanied by compensatory vertical motion.

## Formation

- Convergence at upper level increases the quantity and total weight of air within a limited area. This causes barometric pressure to rise at the surface.
- In the northern hemisphere the surface air circulates anticyclonically round the high pressure area with the usual outflow (divergence) of air across the isobars towards areas of lower pressure.
- This outflowing surface air is replaced only by dry air descending vertically from above. The downward motion of the air is known as 'subsidence'.
- The high pressure system will be maintained so long as the convergence at upper level exceeds the surface divergence.
- When the convergent flow of air at upper level ceases to feed the subsidence the system will decline.

## Some general properties

The air at upper level is dry and is warmed by compressional heating as it subsides into regions of higher pressure. Thus in the central area of a well-developed anticyclone the air at a height of 500 metres is generally warmer than the air below. This increase of air temperature with height is called an inversion and is a very stable condition, in which any vertical ascent of air is arrested at a low level. Since ascending air is one essential condition for the formation of cloud and rain, it follows that the central area of an anticyclone is generally associated with fine dry weather.

## Types of anticyclone

Anticyclones can be classified into two types; cold anticyclones and warm anticyclones. The classification is based upon the temperature of the surface air.

### Cold anticyclones

Cold anticyclones are ones in which the air is colder than the air in the surrounding area. They build up over large land masses in winter, notably over Siberia where the pressure may reach 1,050 hPa or more, but less frequently over the continent of North America.

The process of formation is the reverse to that of a thermal low and may be described therefore as a **thermal high** in which the air becomes cooled through a long period in a cold region. The column of air over the cold surface contracts vertically leaving a deficiency of air at upper level (an upper low). The resultant inflow increases the total quantity and weight of air in the area and barometric pressure increases at surface level. (See Figure 15.1.) The layer of cold air produced is very shallow and lies in the lowest 3 to 4 kilometres. Above this level the air is at 'normal' temperatures. This means that these anticyclones do not appear on higher level charts.

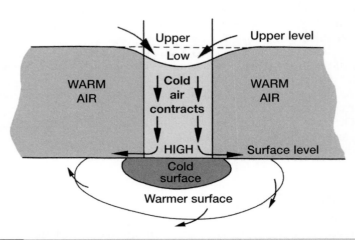

**Fig 15.1** A 'cold' anticyclone.

In late winter, a ridge of high pressure protruding from the Siberian high can give easterly winds over the British Isles and sometimes a prolonged period of intensely cold weather. If the air is dry the weather will be clear, bright and frosty but if enough moisture is picked up from over the North Sea it will be dull and foggy.

## Transitory cold anticyclones

These commonly form within a polar maritime air mass in the temperate latitudes and in the rear of a family of depressions. Weak ones sometimes develop into intense centres when they move over cold land in the winter. In the summer such systems are generally short-lived.

An anticyclone or ridge separating successive depressions of a family normally moves with the depressions.

In winter, near coasts where the air is moist, layer type cloud spreads below the subsidence inversion and accumulates smoke pollution and dust causing **anticyclonic gloom**, particularly in and near large industrial areas. Under these conditions artificial light is sometimes necessary during daylight hours in order to carry on with normal work indoors. Inland, where the air is drier, clear skies at night can cause intense radiation cooling and there is every likelihood of frost or radiation fog.

## Warm anticyclones

These are anticyclones in which the surface is warmer than the surrounding air but at higher levels the air in these anticyclones is actually colder than the surrounding environment at corresponding levels. These features can be identified on charts through the full depth of the troposphere. These anti-cyclones are formed by the air motion in the upper atmosphere.

## Permanent warm anticyclones

These are the oceanic highs in the sub-tropical belts. These systems are very stable and the weather is generally fine with little or no cloud and good visibility. Their average seasonal movement, north and south with the sun, lies somewhere between latitudes 30° and 40° in both hemispheres; but the mean positions of the centres for any particular month vary considerably from year to year. The subtropical highs are the source regions of the tropical maritime air flowing into higher latitudes to meet the polar front.

When the Azores high is well developed and extends well to the north of its average summer latitude we are likely to have a very fine and settled summer in the British Isles so long as the situation is maintained. Conversely, if the high is relatively weak and positioned in a lower than average latitude for the season, our summer will probably be very unsettled with many invading depressions and more than average rainfall.

## Temporary warm anticyclones

These may reach Great Britain as ridges moving along the northern perimeter of the Azores high, or sometimes as separate centres which start as ridges and then break off from the main system. In the British Isles they are more a feature of summer than winter and can persist for long periods.

Temporary warm anticyclones may also develop as a result of continued subsidence within a temporary cold high which remains stationary for a long period.

A warm high often gives bright fine weather, especially over land in summer. There is a possibility of sea fog at any time of the year especially in the spring and early summer. In autumn and winter light winds of maritime origin can bring radiation fog.

## QUESTIONS

1  Describe (with the aid of a diagram) the circulation of air resulting in upper convergence.

2  Describe, in sequence, the processes which result in the formation of an anticyclone.

3  Differentiate between warm and cold anticyclones.

4  Explain how a large anticyclone may govern the speed and direction of movement of a depression.

5  Describe the general properties of an anticyclone.

# 16 TROPICAL REVOLVING STORMS

A tropical revolving storm (TRS) is a disturbance originating in the tropics. It is smaller in size than a temperate latitude depression and usually of far greater intensity; the isobars are nearer to true circles; the pressure gradient is very steep and there are no fronts.

WMO now categorises tropical disturbances as follows, based upon the strength of the winds associated with the storm:

| | |
|---|---|
| **Tropical depression** | Beaufort Force 7 or less |
| **Moderate tropical storm** | Beaufort Force 8 and 9 |
| **Severe tropical storm** | Beaufort Force 10 and 11 |
| **Hurricane** | Beaufort Force 12 |

These storms can blow with incredible fury and raise mountainous seas; their extreme violence and destructive capacity are difficult to realise without experience. The near vicinity of the centre presents the mariner with the most dangerous and dramatic weather conditions he is likely to encounter. They occur in all oceans but are extremely rare in the South Atlantic.

The following notes are only general and it is important to remember that every TRS is different in regard to size, intensity and behaviour; the tracks and rate of travel vary with the general pressure distribution at the time of the occurrence.

## The birth and life of a tropical storm

### Origin

Tropical revolving storms form mostly on the western sides of the oceans. They appear to require a water temperature of 26°C (80°F) in order to form. They generally form between the latitudes of 8° and 20° north and south of the equator. They do not form within 5° of the equator because Coriolis force is too small in these latitudes and a circulation cannot develop. TRS develop from pre-existing or 'seedling' disturbances such as easterly waves (a type of trough) or clusters of clouds associated with the Intertropical Convergence Zone.

## Tracks

After forming, tropical cyclones generally travel westerly then north-westerly or south-westerly, according to hemisphere (see Figure 16.1), recurving in about 20° or more of latitude and then moving off towards the north-east in the northern hemisphere and south-east in southern latitudes. The point of recurvature which is the most western point on the track is also called the *vertex*. (Do not confuse with **vortex** which is the centre of the storm). This broad pattern of movement is by no means regular; it is sometimes very erratic. (See Figures 16.1 to 16.4.)

The tracks vary considerably and depend on the general pressure distribution existing at the time. They tend to curve round the adjacent subtropical anticyclone. An area of high pressure blocking the path can, if of sufficient intensity, cause the storm to change its path. Seasonal migration of the subtropical highs cause a corresponding north and south movement of the average latitude of the vertex.

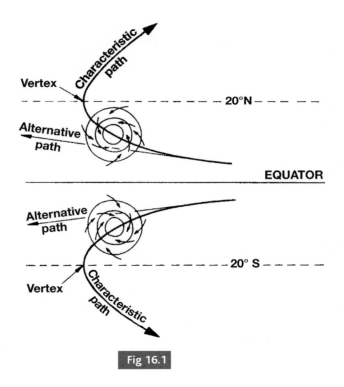

Fig 16.1

Figures 16.2, 16.3 and 16.4 show some typical tracks of tropical revolving storms. Note that recurvature sometimes fails to take place. Occasionally a storm will curve right round so as to form a small loop in the track and then continue along the original path. If two storms are in close proximity they may interact and rotate around each other.

When a storm crosses the coast onto dry land it generally tends to die out rapidly from lack of moisture, but not always. For example, Bay of Bengal cyclones sometimes move across India and regenerate over the Arabian Sea as a fresh moisture supply becomes available. Storms from the China Sea may cross the land into the Bay of Bengal.

Some storms reach into temperate latitudes by which time they will have increased in size and lost much of their original intensity, they may then assume the general characteristics of a temperate latitude depression complete with fronts, or they may become absorbed in the circulation of a frontal depression. The lifetime of a tropical cyclone may vary from a couple of days to over a fortnight.

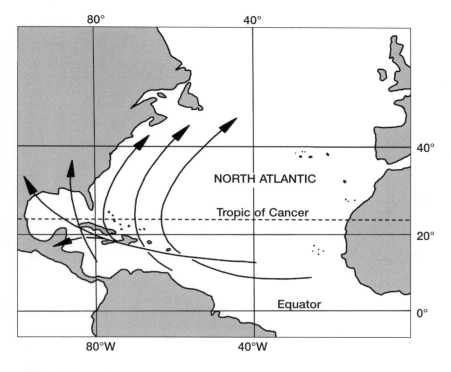

**Fig 16.2** *Some typical tracks of tropical revolving storms.*

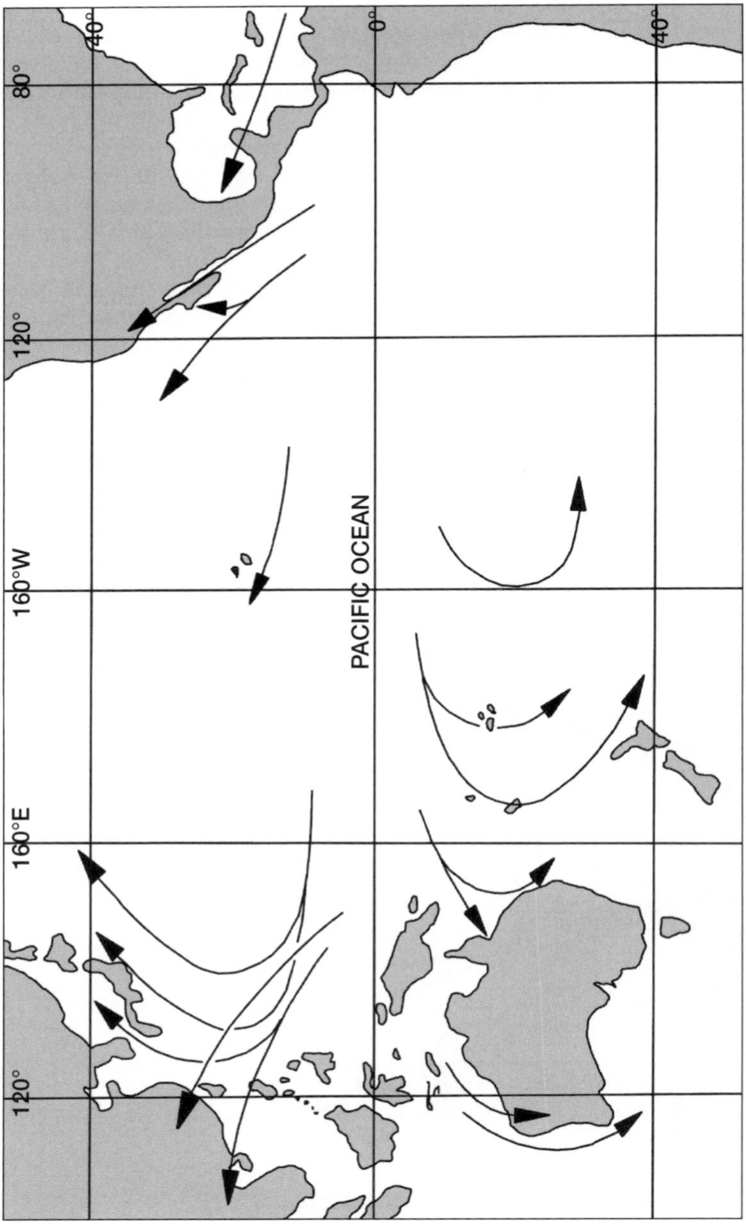

Fig 16.3　Some typical tracks of tropical revolving storms.

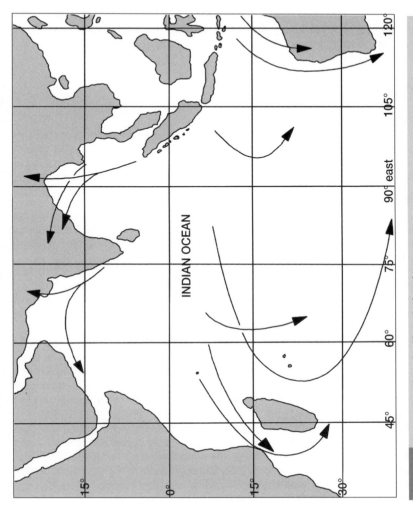

**Fig 16.4** *Some typical tracks of tropical cyclones.*

## Speed of progress

This varies with different storms and the average for each locality also varies a little. In general, speed is slow at first and gradually increases to 10 or 12 knots. During recurvature they slow down, more so if the curve is sharp; sometimes they may become stationary or nearly stationary for a time. After recurvature speed increases to over 20 knots and considerably more if they reach temperate latitudes.

# Tropical storm features

## Pressure

Very few observations have been obtained from the centres of these storms but something in the nature of 960 hPa is likely at the centre of a violent storm, though much lower readings have been recorded. The hurricane force winds are the result of a very steep pressure gradient, not the actual pressure.

## Wind force and direction

From the mariner's viewpoint the wind force and the height of the waves are the significant features of a tropical cyclone. The pressure gradient is generally very steep within about 100 miles from the centre – something like 10 hPa in 50 miles and increasing as the centre is approached.

Wind force varies considerably with different storms. The winds are strongest on that side of the storm which is nearest the adjacent subtropical high, because the cyclonic circulation (ie anticlockwise in the northern hemisphere and clockwise in the southern hemisphere) is reinforced by the general airstream in which the storm is moving. Thus the strongest winds occur in the right-hand semicircle in the northern hemisphere and in the left-hand semicircle in the southern hemisphere. In the centre itself there is a small circular area (of anything up to as much as 40 miles in diameter) called the **eye** or the **vortex** in which there are light variable winds, patches of blue sky visible between broken low clouds and a mountainous confused sea. (See Figure 17.2. See also under **Weather**.)

Around the calm central eye lies a ring of very strong winds which is known as the **eyewall**. Beyond the eyewall the winds decay towards the outer limits of the storm. At a range of 200 miles the wind force may reduce to Force 6 or 7, with correspondingly smaller waves, although there will probably be a very heavy swell, particularly on the path in advance of the storm.

Very heavy rain is a feature of all tropical revolving storms.

Near the vortex the angle of indraft (see Glossary) is smallest, being only slightly aslant the isobars, whilst at a distance of about 200 miles from the centre the wind may be across the isobars at an angle of 45°.

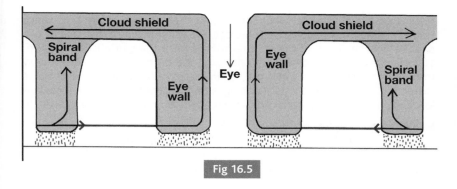

Fig 16.5

## Cloud sequence

In a TRS the cloud sequence is normally in the form of cirrus, altostratus, cumulus fractus, scud and nimbostratus until the eye is reached, when there will be a partly clear sky.

## Weather

Very heavy rain is a feature of all tropical revolving storms, it usually commences to fall as light rain at a distance of about 100 to 150 miles from the centre. As the centre approaches, torrential rain, hurricane force winds with extremely violent squalls and sudden shifts of wind are experienced, sometimes with thunder and lightning. The sea becomes exceptionally high and is covered with froth and flying spray which mingles with the rain and fills the air with water; visibility is thus very seriously impaired. The deafening roar, which accompanies this weather close to the centre, will drown the noise of any thunderstorm.

Large seaworthy ships are liable to become unmanageable in such conditions and may sustain heavy damage.

As the edge of the eye passes the wind suddenly becomes light, the rain ceases, the seas become mountainous and confused so that they approach from all directions. Blue sky is often visible between broken patches of low cloud. The roar of the wind and sea fades towards the centre of the eye. The opposite side of the eye arrives with the same loud roar and the sudden onslaught of violent winds strikes from the opposite direction to that previously experienced.

The weather in the rear of the storm is generally less extensive and passes more quickly than on the forward side. As the TRS moves towards the shore, the interaction with other weather systems may produce tornadoes.

## Storm tides

The long swell ahead of a tropical cyclone is sometimes experienced at a distance of more than 1,000 miles from the storm's centre. It travels much faster than the storm itself and, not infrequently, causes a 'storm tide' which results in disastrous flooding on the coast. The water begins to rise one or two days before the arrival of the storm – that is when the storm is from 300 to 500 miles away – and continues to rise until the storm passes or curves away from the area. The rise of water may be in excess of 6 metres (18 feet) above the predicted level. The coastal flooding is particularly severe where a coast is low lying and when the storm tide arrives at the time of a high spring tide.

## Size of tropical cyclones

Diameters vary from 50 to 1,000 miles and are rarely less than 50 or more than 500; more often than not they are over 100 miles. A storm generally increases its area as it progresses along its path.

## Seasons

These storms develop during the warmest months of the year. Generally this is in late summer and early autumn of the appropriate hemisphere. In monsoon areas the storms tend to occur at the inter-monsoon periods. (See Figure 16.6.)

## Formation of tropical cyclones

As yet, the process of the formation of these storms is not completely understood but research continues and some of the conditions which are known to be favourable are given below.

(a) It is essential that a weak cyclonic circulation should exist locally a short time beforehand; this can occur only in latitudes where the Earth's rotation is effective (ie never less than 5° from the equator).
(b) An adequate supply of moisture in a deep, warm layer of unstable air (see Chapter 4). The sea surface temperature must be at least 26°C (80°F). These essential conditions exist mainly towards the end of the hottest seasons.
(c) Little change in wind direction with height in the lower levels of the troposphere.

## Nomenclature

Tropical revolving storms are known by local names in different parts of the world and these names are given in Figure 16.6.

# Notes on TRS behaviour in various regions

## West Indies and North Atlantic

These hurricanes develop in the doldrum area (Intertropical Convergence Zone) which, at the beginning of the season (June) and end of the season (November),

| Region | Local name | Season | Worst months |
|---|---|---|---|
| North Atlantic | Hurricane | June to November | September |
| South Atlantic | Extremely rare | | |
| Arabian Sea | Cyclone | April to July and September to January | Change of monsoon: May and June, October and November |
| Bay of Bengal* | Cyclone | April to December but have been recorded in all months | June, July, October and November |
| Western North Pacific and China Sea | Typhoon (Baguios in Philippines) | All months (mainly July to November) | July, August and September |
| Eastern North Pacific | Hurricane | June to November | September |
| Western South Pacific | Hurricane | December to April | January, February and March |
| South Indian Ocean | Cyclone | November to April | January and February |
| North-West Australia | Cyclone | December to April | January and February |

Fig 16.6

* Worst months refer to wind force, not frequency. Months in which storms occur most frequently are from July to October (inclusive).

117

is found mostly in the Caribbean, while at the middle of the season the area extends to the Cape Verde Islands. The track of these storms is 'steered' by the position and extent of the permanent North Atlantic anticyclone; if it extends to the American coast a storm may perhaps not recurve but go right through the Caribbean and cross the United States coastline. Normally, however, the hurricanes recurve to the north and east round the western extremity of the anticyclone. Most of the southern coast of the Caribbean is not directly affected by these storms. It is not uncommon for a hurricane to skirt the United States coastline well beyond New York. The average rate of progress of the hurricanes is about 300 miles per day and their average life is about six days. During the worst month (September) the average number of storms which reached hurricane force during an 80 year period was two.

## Arabian Sea

The areas in which these cyclones originate depends on the monsoon season. During the SW monsoon (April to July) it is near the Maldive Islands (5°–10°N, 65°–75°E); in the NE monsoon season it moves to the vicinity of the Laccadive Isles (9°–14°N, 70°–75°E). Occasional storms enter the Arabian Sea from the Bay of Bengal via Sri Lanka. The tracks of all these cyclones are very variable; their average rate of progress is about 7 knots. In the worst months of each season (May/June and October/November), during a 66 year period, there was an average of one storm every two years.

## Bay of Bengal

The birthplace of these cyclones is also governed by the monsoon season and tends to move with the sun. During the SW monsoon they are generally born somewhere near the Nicobar Islands (6°–9°N, 92°–94°E) in April and north of 16°N in June; in the NE monsoon season their birthplace has moved south to about 12°N by November. Some typhoons from the western North Pacific enter the Bay via the Thai/Malay Peninsular area. Tracks of storms in the Bay of Bengal tend to go to the NW and N; they may also go due W or even to eastward. In each of the worst months (October and November) during a 61 year period there was about one violent storm (ie reaching Force 12) per year; during the lesser maximum period (June and July) there was only about one every two years.

## Western North Pacific and China Sea*

This is by far the most active region for tropical storms. Most of them are born somewhere between the Philippines (about 125°E) and the Marshall Islands (170°E), between 5°N and 20°N; a very large area to choose from. Although

*Note. At the end of Chapter 17 reference is made to special features of tropical storms in China Sea and Western North Pacific and also in the South Indian Ocean.

these typhoons generally tend to follow a conventional track (NW, N and then NE), they sometimes behave quite erratically and some of them travel about WNW and may enter the Bay of Bengal overland. Their rate of progress might be anything between 10 and 20 knots. In the worst months (July to September) during a 70 year period there was an average of about four storms per month over the whole area.

## Eastern North Pacific

Most of the hurricanes here originate between about 120°W and the Central American coast, between about 10° and 30°N. Their tracks generally follow the coastline more or less in a NW'ly direction but they may go to the westward. The storm field is usually rather small; their rate of progress might be about 10 knots. In this area the mariner may have little or no warning of a storm's approach, the usual indications (see Chapter 17) being sometimes absent, especially during the season of bad weather (June to November). In the worst month, September, during an 18 year period, the average number of storms recorded was about two per annum, but a total of only 7.4 per annum for all months together.

## South Indian Ocean

The season for these cyclones (November to April) coincides with the NE monsoon in the Arabian Sea which becomes a NW wind after crossing the Equator. The cyclones are born in the doldrums between this NW monsoon wind and the SE Trade wind area, somewhere between Southern Sumatra (about 100°E) and Malagache (Madagascar) (about 50°E) and between 7° and 12°S. They cover, therefore, a very large stretch of ocean; fortunately they tend to follow conventional tracks (SW, S and then SE). Their rate of progress is about 8 knots normally. During the worst months (January and February) during a 100 year period, the average number of storms was about eight per annum, most of which occurred to the west of longitude 80°E.

## North-west Australia

The Arafura Sea, due north of Australia, is the usual breeding ground for cyclones, though sometimes they are born in the Timor Sea area. They normally follow a conventional track (SW, S and then SE) and occasionally they reach as far south as the Australian Bight. In the worst months (January and February) the average is not more than one per annum.

## South Pacific

There are no tropical storms in the eastern South Pacific. In the western part of the ocean the hurricanes originate somewhere in the enormous area between 160°E (south of the Solomon Islands) and 140°W (Marquesas Isles) and between 5° and 20°S. They may be born as far west as the Coral Sea (about 150°E). They tend to follow a conventional track (SW, S and then SE);

sometimes they reach the Australian coast. Their speed of advance may vary between 10 and 15 knots. In the worst months (January, February and March), during a 105 year period, the average number of recorded storms was about one per month every two years.

## Diurnal variation of atmospheric pressure and indications of the approach of a TRS

See Chapter 17.

### QUESTIONS

1 Draw an annotated diagram of a TRS in the northern hemisphere. Show isobars, wind arrows, track, vertex, eye (or vortex), right- and left-hand semicircles, trough.

2 Discuss in general terms the following aspects in relation to tropical storms: latitude of origin, tracks, latitude of vertex, diameter, pressure gradient, wind force and direction, speed of progress, weather, sea and swell.

3 The process of the formation of tropical cyclones is, as yet, not fully understood. Describe those conditions which are known to be essential to the formation of these storms.

4 In which semicircle of a TRS do the strongest winds usually occur? Give a reason for your answer.

5 Describe the winds, weather and state of sea that a stationary observer would probably experience with the approach, passage and retreat of a TRS. Assume the storm's eye is 200 miles distant to start with and that it will pass over the observer's position.

6 Discuss storm tides.

7 List the regions in which tropical revolving storms occur, also the local names of these storms, their seasons and worst months.

8 Draw a sketch map of the North and South Indian Oceans and insert typical tracks of cyclones.

9 Where and in which months of the year do typhoons occur? Which are the worst months?

# 17 AVOIDANCE OF THE WORST EFFECTS OF A TRS

## Warning signs

In any locality during the tropical revolving storm (TRS) season the navigator must exercise constant vigilance to ensure that he is not caught unawares in the path of a storm. Fortunately nature provides warning signs to the alert; also the meteorological services ashore broadcast very valuable warnings by radio (see Admiralty List of Radio Signals Vol 3) whenever it is available from ship and/or other sources.

The mariner's aim must be to avoid getting near the centre of the storm; here again nature provides these storms with certain common features which have enabled the evolvement of guidance 'rules' to help in keeping the ship out of serious trouble.

Except for the behaviour of the barometer, any one of the following warning signs, if taken alone, is only an uncertain indication of the approach of a TRS. Barometer, swell, sky, etc, must be considered together.

### Natural warnings

**The barometer** In temperate latitudes atmospheric pressure is subject to large, rapid and very irregular daily changes caused by the development and movement of travelling weather systems. In the tropics, however, in normal weather, the day to day changes in the readings of the barometer are very small and follow a very regular pattern of diurnal variation: consequently the barometer needs to be corrected for its diurnal variation.

Figure 17.1 shows a typical curve of pressure changes for a day in the tropics. The maxima occur at 1000 and 2200 hours, local time, and the minima at 0400 and 1600 hours. The range of daily change averages 3 hPa (about 0.1 in) at the equator, decreasing with latitude (N and S) to 2.5 hPa at latitude 30° and 1.7 hPa at 35°.

In any region and season when tropical cyclones are likely to occur, no matter how fine and settled the weather may appear, **the barometer should be read and recorded every hour**. The reading, after having being reduced to

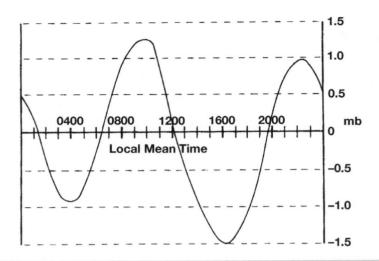

**Fig 17.1** *Diurnal range of pressure in tropics.*

sea level, should then be corrected for diurnal variation. *Each reading thus corrected should be compared with the mean pressure for the locality and season (as shown in the Admiralty Pilot or Meteorological Climatological Atlas) and, if it is 3 hPa or more below the mean pressure, or **if there is a marked departure from the diurnal variation, there is a risk of a TRS forming or developing** and a warning signal should immediately be sent by radio to the nearest coast radio station and repeated to all ships.

If a corrected reading is as low as 5 hPa below normal, it should be taken to mean that a TRS is almost certainly somewhere in the area and probably within 200 miles of the observer.

When the storm is 500 to 1,000 miles away the barometer usually becomes unsteady and often rises a little above the normal. This is followed by a definite slow fall, usually over a distance of 500 to 120 miles from the storm centre, thereafter the rate of fall increases becoming rapid on the near approach of the centre .

**Appearance of sky** Vivid colouring at sunrise and sunset are often a warning feature, accompanied or followed by cirrus cloud, not infrequently in V-shaped formation pointing towards the centre. Cirrus may first appear when the storm

*Caution: When entering a barometric pressure in the logbook, or when including it in a radio weather report, the correction for diurnal variation should NOT be applied. This correction is only for the Master's operational use during the tropical cyclone season in the area.*

is from 300 to 600 miles away and is often the first warning of a TRS, even in the early stages of development. Later there will be altostratus and eventually cumulus fractus and scud.

**Swell** There will be a long swell coming from the direction of the storm centre provided there is no land intervening between the storm and the ship. The swell travels faster than the storm and usually extends more than 400 miles and sometimes 1,000 miles from the centre. Thus it may well be the first warning sign.

**Visibility** Exceptionally good visibility frequently precedes a tropical revolving storm.

**Wind** During the storm season an appreciable increase in wind force and/or direction should be regarded as a possible indication of the approach of a TRS.

## Warning by radar

The average merchant ship's 3 centimetre radar can, in normal propagation conditions, display rain at a maximum range of about 30 miles, so its value in warning of a tropical storm is very limited. Nevertheless, within that range very clear radar screen pictures of the rain belt surrounding the eye (**vortex**) have been seen, the eye itself showing as a dark circular area in the centre. But by this time the ship will have already become heavily involved in the storm. A greater range of detection can be expected with 10 centimetre radar.

## Radio warnings from a meteorological service

All ocean areas which are visited by tropical storms are now covered by radio weather bulletins and storm warnings issued by one or more local meteorological services.

Images from meteorological satellites (see Glossary) provide valuable information about existing storms and their development, and in some areas reconnaissance aircraft keep in contact with each storm.

Provided that the extent, wind force, existing track and speed of movement of a storm are known, detailed warnings can be broadcast to shipping at suitable intervals including forecasts of the storm's probable behaviour. But these storms are born in mid-ocean and, in the absence of ship reports (supplemented by aircraft reports and/or satellite pictures) the meteorologists cannot know of a storm's existence. This is recognised by the International Convention for Safety of Life at Sea which requires the master of any ship who suspects the existence of a tropical storm to report it.

With the advent of the Global Maritime Distress and Safety Systems (GMDSS) a large proportion of ships no longer carry qualified radio officers. Information concerning meteorological warnings, including that relating to TRS is principally conveyed now by telex or navtex. This emphasises the responsibility of the master and ship's officers to report any likely indications.

## Master's action when storm suspected or known to exist

Article 35 of the International Convention for Safety of Life at Sea calls for a safety message to be sent as soon as possible to the nearest authority ashore and broadcast to shipping in the vicinity. Such a message might read:

**Storm warning**
Typhoon seems to be developing. 0840 GMT. August 15. 0635N, 133°20'E. Barometer corrected 1,000 hectopascals, tendency down 3 hectopascals. Wind NW Force 4. Moderate westerly swell. Cirrus clouds. Course 345, 15 knots.

Similar reports should be sent at intervals of not more than three hours until the ship is clear of the storm.

It is in the interest of the reporting ship and all other ships that weather reports be sent also to meteorological authorities at frequent intervals. Normal seamanlike precautions should be taken on board for exceptionally rough weather.

## Practical rules for avoiding the worst of a tropical storm

As the isobars in a tropical revolving storm are always circular in shape the storm field has two semicircles which, for safety purposes, are classified as 'dangerous' and 'navigable'. (See Figure 17.2.)

### The dangerous semicircle

This is the right-hand one in the northern hemisphere and the left-hand one in the southern latitudes. It is termed dangerous because the winds therein tend to blow a ship into the path of the advancing storm's centre, or the storm might recurve and the centre pass over the ship. The advance quadrant of this semicircle is particularly dangerous.

### The navigable semicircle

Here the winds tend to blow the ship towards the rear of the path, and it lies on that side of the path which is away from the direction in which a storm usually recurves.

**Before deciding on evasive action** the master needs to know:

1 The bearing of the storm's centre.
2 If possible the distance from the centre.
3 The semicircle in which the ship is located.
4 The likely path of the storm.

## 1 Find the bearing of the centre

Use Buys Ballot's Law (see page 45 and Glossary). Remember the wind crosses the isobars at an angle of about 45° at the edge of the storm field, decreasing until nearly parallel with the isobars near the centre. Face the wind and the centre is on your right in the northern hemisphere and on your left in the southern hemisphere. Allow about 12 compass points when the corrected barometer reading starts to fall, then 10 points when it has fallen 10 hPa (0.3 in) and 8 points if it falls 20 hPa (0.6 in) or more. The wind direction tends to be erratic during squalls. The best time for observing is when the wind steadies just after a squall.

## 2 Try to estimate the distance from the centre

As a very rough guide, in the absence of detailed meteorological data, the centre would probably be about 200 miles away if the corrected barometer reading is 5 hPa (0.15 in) below the local normal and the wind force is about 6. If the wind force is 8 the centre is probably within 100 miles.

## 3 Find out in which semicircle the ship is located

To a stationary observer in either hemisphere, the wind shifts to the right in the right-hand semicircle and to the left in the left-hand semicircle. Therefore to eliminate the relative motion problem between ship and storm, the master should **heave-to** or **stop the ship** to find out the true windshift and thus determine the semicircle .

If the wind veers the ship is in the right-hand semicircle; if it backs she is in the left-hand semicircle; if it is steady in direction she is in the direct path of the storm.

The barometer falls ahead of the trough and rises in the rear, thus the quadrant can also be determined.

## 4 Try to find the likely path of the storm

Provided the ship is either stopped or hove-to, a very rough estimate of the storm's probable path can be made by working out two bearings of the centre (as described earlier) with an interval of about three hours between them. The storm is unlikely to be decreasing its latitude and, if the latitude is less than 20° it is unlikely to be making any movement towards the east.

A diagram similar to Figure 17.2 (but omitting the ship) on a piece of tracing paper will be found useful here in deciding what action to take.

The answers to all the above questions will be very greatly facilitated if official information about the storm's behaviour has been received by radio from a meteorological service.

## Action to avoid the worst of the storm: northern hemisphere

**Right-hand or 'dangerous' semicircle** (Figure 17.2. *Ship A*). If under power proceed with maximum practical speed with wind ahead or on starboard bow, hauling round to starboard as the wind veers. If sea room is inadequate to make headway, or if the ship is under sail only, then heave-to on starboard tack.

**Left-hand or 'navigable' semicircle** (Figure 17.2. *Ship B*). Run with the wind well on the starboard quarter (whether under power or sail) making all possible

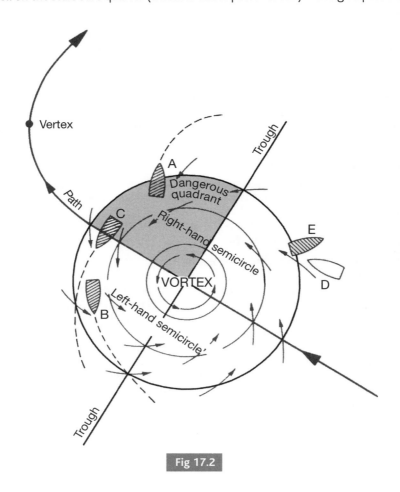

Fig 17.2

speed and haul round to port as the wind backs. If sea room is insufficient to make headway, heave-to on whichever tack is considered to be the safest under existing circumstances and conditions.

**In direct path and ahead of storm** (Figure 17.2. *Ship C*). With the wind on the starboard quarter make all possible speed into the navigable semicircle. If inadequate sea room to do this, it may be preferable to proceed into the dangerous semicircle rather than stay in the direct path, but be on the alert for possible recurvature.

**Vessel overtaking the storm** (Figure 17.2. *Ship D*). This may not be unusual in the fast ships of today. Heave-to; the wind will then shift to the right and the barometer will rise showing that Ship D is in the rear quadrant of the dangerous semicircle. She should then get the wind on the starboard bow (*Ship E*) and allow the storm to get clear.

If Ship D does not heave-to when the storm is first suspected and continues on course, the barometer will fall and the wind will shift to the left. This can lead to an erroneous assumption that she is in the left-hand semicircle ahead of the trough; if she then proceeds (obeying the rules) with the wind on the starboard quarter she may run into the dangerous quadrant, especially if her original course was converging with the path.

## Southern hemisphere – action

Exactly the same principles apply as in the northern hemisphere, but because the wind circulates clockwise the left-hand semicircle is the 'dangerous' one and the right-hand one is 'navigable'. Thus the action to be taken to keep the ship clear of the worst of the storm is different, as summarised below.

**Left-hand or 'dangerous' semicircle** (Figure 17.3. *Ship F*). If under power proceed at maximum practicable speed with the wind ahead or on port bow hauling round as the wind backs. If impracticable to make headway, heave-to on the port tack.

**Right-hand 'navigable' semicircle** (Figure 17.3. *Ship G*). Run with the wind on the port quarter making all possible speed and hauling round to starboard as the wind veers. If impracticable to make headway, heave-to in the most comfortable position.

**On the storm path ahead of the centre** (Figure 17.3. *Ship H*). With the wind on the port quarter make all possible speed into the navigable semicircle. If there is insufficient sea room for this, act as described for northern hemisphere.

**Vessel overtaking the storm** (Figure 17.3. *Ship J*). Heave-to; the windshift to the left and rising barometer will show Ship J to be in the rear quadrant of the dangerous semicircle. Get the wind on the port bow (*Ship K*).

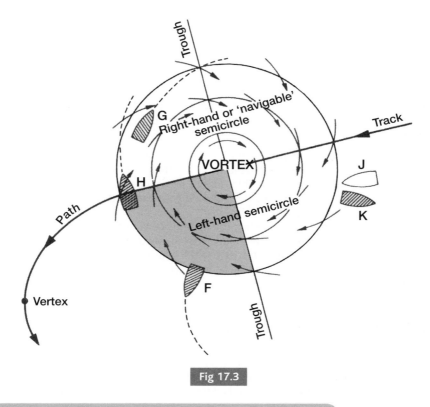

**Fig 17.3**

## Use of safety sectors – additional precaution

The following procedure is only possible when accurate, regular radio reports of the storm's progress are available (refer to Figure 17.4).

**1** On the chart, plot the reported position of the storm's centre (A).

**2** From A lay off the track and distance the centre is expected to make during the next 24 hours (AB).

**3** With A (the eye) as centre and radius AB construct an 80° sector (with 40° on each side of the track). This will be sector 1 in Figure 17.4 (refer to N hemisphere).

**4** Endeavour to keep the ship outside this sector which is a 'dangerous' area.

**5** Each time the storm alters its direction of movement, lay off a new sector.

The normal 'rules' for avoiding the worst of a TRS must still be adhered to in principle.

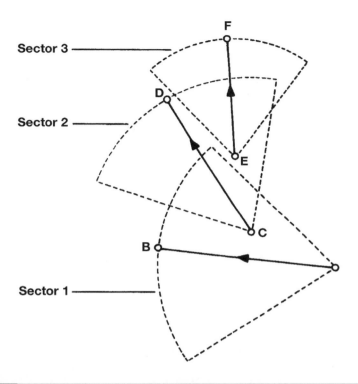

**Fig 17.4** *A, C and E are successive positions of the storm's centre as reported by radio and the expected tracks are AB, CD and EF.*

## Ship in harbour

When in harbour, whether lying alongside or at anchor, during a tropical storm season or period, vigilance must be maintained as at sea. Barometer, wind and sky need watching carefully and it is desirable, if practicable, to set a modified radio listening watch for weather bulletins.

If a storm is threatened, early seamanlike precautions must be taken. If it seems likely that the storm centre will pass nearby it may be best to proceed to sea, provided there is plenty of sea room available. If remaining in harbour and at anchor there is the likelihood of having to use main engines and/or to let go a second anchor. Buoying the anchors with brightly painted buoys might well facilitate their successful use for this purpose.

A small ship at sea within access of a suitable harbour may benefit by seeking shelter rather than remaining at sea.

## Local peculiarities of tropical storms

### China Sea and western North Pacific

If there is a fairly steady south-west or north-west wind in June to September in the northern part of the China Sea, a typhoon to the northward is probable, the reason being that there is no season when these winds are normally common; even the south-west monsoon is usually from the south or south-east.

### South Indian Ocean

An approaching cyclone may be masked by the SE trade wind; should the trade wind approach gale force the ship should be hove-to so as to observe the wind-shift.

In all tropical revolving storm areas storm behaviour may be very erratic.

---

### QUESTIONS

1. (a) Explain why the 'dangerous' and 'navigable' semicircles of a TRS are so named.
   (b) Which is the 'dangerous' semicircle in a TRS of the southern hemisphere?

2. Explain why, when you find yourself in the vicinity of a tropical cyclone, you should stop your ship or heave-to *before* deciding what action you should take to avoid the storm.

3. (a) On a voyage from Sydney, Australia, to Fiji, you observe the warning signs of the approach of a hurricane. Describe how you would estimate the bearing of the storm's centre, the quadrant in which your ship is located, the probable path of the storm and your distance from the vortex.
   (b) What action should be taken if found to be
      (i) in the dangerous quadrant or
      (ii) in the direct path of the storm?

4. List the signs which would indicate the probable approach of a TRS.

5. Tropical cyclones form mostly on the western side of the oceans. Why is this so?

6. What action must a ship's master take in accordance with Article 35 of the International Convention of Safety of Life at Sea, when the presence of a TRS is suspected or known to exist?

ospheric pressure within

maximum and minimum

ropical cyclones may be
eadings must be further
State where the normal
range for any particular

approaching from the north.
weather you would probably
sses
nd

which is travelling north. There
and there is no available shelter.
why.

N, longitude 70°W, bound from
se of 240°. Warning is received of
a Strait and which is moving NE.
and give reasons for your answer.

how safety sectors should be used
S. Assume that regular radio reports
eing received.

# 18 WEATHER FORECASTING FOR THE SEAFARER

## Weather forecasting

The term forecast was coined in its meteorological sense by Admiral Fitzroy when he first attempted to anticipate the weather and to issue visual storm warnings in about 1860. It was a wise and prudent choice of a word, for even today with the wide network of observations, speedy communications and long experience, aided by the high speed computer and satellite pictures, the weather forecaster can only attain reasonable accuracy at about 24 hours ahead. Owing to the frequency at which forecasts are broadcast this modest attainment is of enormous value for the safety and economy of shipping and it is fortunate for the mariner that wind, the most significant parameter, is not a very difficult one to forecast.

### The synoptic map

The basic tool of the weather forecaster is and always has been the synoptic map, which gives a synopsis, or bird's-eye view, of the factors which make up the existing weather over as wide an area as possible and this implies good communications in particular.

Before Marconi came on the scene only the electric telegraph was available, so the network was limited to land areas. The introduction of wireless telegraphy in 1901 enabled weather reports to be received from ships at sea. The structure of the modern surface weather map goes back to the First World War, when the frontal theory of meteorology was generally accepted.

The international network of upper air observations of pressure, humidity, temperature and wind, to a height of about 10,000 metres, enabling upper air maps to be prepared, was started soon after the Second World War. Now we have observations of cloud cover, extent of sea ice, etc, from weather satellites and we also have the high speed computer, all of which are of great help to meteorologists in their attempts to attain accurate forecasts.

## Preparation

All synoptic weather observations are transmitted in a simple international code which transcends all language barriers, and the method of preparing the resultant map is also international; thus a Russian or a Chinese person can readily understand a British synoptic map and vice versa. In fact there is a regular exchange of up-to-date weather maps. The observations forming the basis of the four main synoptic maps each day are made on a rigid time schedule: 0000, 0600, 1200 and 1800 GMT. Many hundreds of observations are thus received regularly by the relevant meteorological services in each region and are then re-transmitted for the benefit of all those requiring them, the observations having been provided from a fixed network of shore stations, from ships at sea and from aircraft in flight, plus the upper air observations from a much more widely spaced network.

Observations are fed into a computer model of the atmosphere and this produces both analysis and forecast charts.

## Special meteorological services for shipping

Because international meteorology was born out of the Maritime Conference at Brussels in 1853 and since then most of the oceans' weather observations have come from merchant ships, it is not surprising that meteorological services have for many years done their best to help shipping by providing forecasts and essential climatological information. Nowadays almost all ocean and coastal areas are covered by radio weather bulletins of one kind or another.

The earliest information available for shipping was solely climatological plus ocean current maps compiled from the data in ships' logbooks. This was transformed by the advent of wireless telegraphy in the twentieth century which now meant that ships could transmit weather observations to shore and the converse, that weather bulletins could be broadcast to shipping for specific ocean areas. Both World Wars heightened the importance of meterological information for military purposes and the first bulletins were issued from 1919 onwards, these relating to the North Atlantic. Since 1948 each meteorological service with a seaboard is responsible for the issue of standard bulletins covering designated and published areas.

## Storm warnings

Until the 1980s Fitzroy's visual storm warnings consisting of the north or south cone for winds with a northerly or southerly component respectively were still exhibited at the few remaining coastguard stations and at a few ports, when winds of Force 8 and above were expected. In June 1984 they were discontinued because it is considered almost certain that all vessels likely to proceed offshore nowadays are fitted with radio and are able to receive the relatively frequent and comprehensive forecasts and warnings with which modern seafarers are so familiar. More elaborate visual signals are exhibited in certain countries, for example in the United States and the typhoon warnings in Hong Kong.

Under the WMO scheme, every radio weather bulletin for shipping, whether it be for ocean areas or coastal waters, includes warnings of gales (Force 8 and above) and storms (Force 10 and above) when either of these is anticipated. In tropical areas, during the cyclonic storm season, special steps are taken to give very early warning of the approach and development of such storms; if the warnings are transmitted at unscheduled times they are repeated in the routine bulletins.

## Radio bulletins for shipping

Under an international scheme prepared by the WMO, practically all ocean areas are today covered by radio weather bulletins for shipping on the high seas. The bulletins are presented in a more or less standard form so that they are readily understood, the text being in the language of the issuing country and English. In a few cases a simple code may be used. The contents of these bulletins are in compliance with the International Convention for Safety of Life at Sea in association with the WMO and they are designed to give the maximum of essential information as briefly as possible. In some cases more than one nation issues bulletins for the same area; this is not necessarily a handicap: if more than one bulletin gives a similar forecast the mariner can have more confidence in it. Bulletins for coastal areas are commonly broadcast by R/T or on domestic broadcast — often at fairly frequent intervals and their contents are often somewhat briefer. Details of all bulletins for shipping are given in the Admiralty List of Radio Signals, Vol 3.

## Forecasts

Every radio bulletin for shipping, whether it be for ocean or coastal areas contains, in addition to gale and storm warnings, a forecast of the expected wind, weather and visibility for the next 24 hours, for the various sections of the area concerned. In some areas (eg off Iceland and in the Baltic) warning of sub-freezing air temperature is given. Usually the forecast is preceded by a brief statement of the existing weather systems in the area and their expected movement and development.

## Details of the weather bulletins

Many of the larger oceans are subdivided into sections to facilitate descriptions of the actual and forecast weather. For example, the UK authorities divide the Eastern Atlantic outside coastal areas into six standard sections.

## Actual weather reports

Most bulletins for the high seas and some for coastal areas contain reports of existing weather conditions at a selection of ships and/or shore stations. These reports include wind direction and force, weather, visibility, barometric pressure and, sometimes, wave data from the ships. These data are included to give the mariner an overall picture of the situation in as wide an area as practicable.

### The use of radio facsimile aboard ship

Radio facsimile maps are broadcast by several meteorological services and the frequencies used are such that they can be received aboard any ship with a suitable receiver. Some fax machines can be set for automatic reception. The machine is then switched on and off by a pulse received at the beginning and end of the chart transmission. Details of the charts available and transmission schedules can be obtained from the Admiralty List of Radio Signals, Vol 3. A wide selection of weather maps is available by radio fax. Analysis charts are produced every six hours and prognostic charts are available for 24, 48 and 72 hours. Times and types of charts available depend upon the transmitting stations. Charts can be received which detail sea surface temperature, the extent and type of sea ice and the position and strength of surface currents. These charts, together with charts detailing sea and swell heights, can be used for route planning.

### Special advice on request

Most meteorological services are willing to give special advice about impending weather in a particular area on request, by phone or radio.

### Climatological information

Much information about climatic conditions in various parts of the world's ocean and coastal waters is given in the Admiralty Pilots. This has been largely compiled from data shown in climatic atlases prepared by meteorological services from observations made aboard merchant ships.

### International aspects of meteorology

The weather recognises no frontiers. Every country needs as accurate information as possible about the present and future weather, not only for the safety of all forms of transport and for a variety of industrial and economic purposes, but also for agriculture, sport and tourism. This involves the rapid receipt of regular observations from numerous locations in various countries and oceanic areas. It is not surprising therefore that international co-operation in the science of meteorology has a long and outstanding history of success.

## Meteorological organisations

It was a seaman, Lieut Maury of the US Navy, who took the initiative when he inspired and organised the first International Conference on Maritime Meteorology at Brussels in 1853. It seems quite natural that international meteorology should have this maritime origin because weather directly affects the safety, comfort and prosperity of the mariner more than almost anybody else. In 1855, as a result of the Brussels Conference, the British Meteorological Office was born, its first director being another seaman, Admiral Fitzroy. Its function was to collect the observations from ships at sea for compiling meteorological atlases and to collect data about surface currents of the oceans and other phenomena for the benefit of shipping. Under Fitzroy's direction a visual storm warning service for shipping was started and a rudimentary forecast service. In 1873, resulting from an international conference at Leipzig, at which the directors of most of the then meteorological services were present, the International Meteorological Organisation (IMO) was founded. This was a more or less unofficial body, its function being to co-ordinate all meteorological activities on a worldwide basis and it proved very successful. In 1951 the IMO was transformed into the World Meteorological Organisation (WMO), an official inter-governmental body and specialised agency of the United Nations; about 178 countries are members at present.

### Functions and strucures of the WMO

The main purpose of the WMO is to arrange, internationally:

❖ Networks of observing stations and the requisite communication facilities.
❖ Standardisation of observing practice and meteorological codes and publication of statistics.
❖ The most effective application of meteorology to shipping, aviation, agriculture and other human activities.
❖ The encouragement of research and training.

To carry out its work the WMO has a Secretary General and headquarters staff at Geneva under the direction of an Executive Committee of 24 Directors which meets annually. The supreme body is the WMO Congress which meets once every four years. For operational purposes the world is divided into six regions, in each of which the meteorological activity is co-ordinated by a regional association. The technical work of WMO is done by eight Technical Commissions, composed of experts appointed by individual countries; they have four-yearly meetings and do their work between sessions by correspondence. The Commission for Maritime Meteorology, which is in effect the offspring of the 1853 Brussels Conference, looks after all aspects of Maritime Meteorology.

## International meteorology in action

Today every country in the world has a sizeable network of meteorological observing stations, a few of which make upper air observations by radio controlled instruments carried aloft by balloon to a height of about 18,000 metres (60,000 feet). Observations are made at regular intervals and the coded results are immediately transmitted by the quickest means to a national collecting centre, where they are immediately plotted on synoptic weather maps and used for forecasting purposes. At the same time these messages are re-transmitted to other countries and to regional collecting centres whence they are transmitted again for the benefit of countries in other regions. Thus, for example the United Kingdom has the benefit of observations as far away as the Pacific coast of the USA. The codes, maps and plotting procedure are such that a meteorologist of any nationality can readily understand them without interpretation. Today, the weather maps prepared in most countries are broadcast in detail by radio facsimile for the benefit of other countries. Also all countries can easily have available regular images of worldwide meteorological observations (cloud cover, etc) made by satellite.

## The Selected Ship Scheme

The oceans not only occupy three-quarters of the Earth's surface but are also the main source of atmospheric disturbances and of our varied weather generally. Hence the meteorologist has a vital need of regular observations from ocean areas.

The Selected Ship Scheme is international and is run under the auspices of the WMO. Observations are made by the appropriate watchkeeper every six hours, covering barometric pressure, air and sea temperatures, direction and strength of wind, wave heights, current weather, cloud cover and visibility. This information is then coded numerically and is transmitted to designated shore radio stations.

Summarised information about making the observations and about the instruments used is given in Chapter 25. Details are given in *The Marine Observer's Handbook*, which is issued free to all British Selected Ships and can be bought from HM Stationery Office. By taking part in this scheme masters are providing much-needed help to the meteorologist in the job of providing forecasts for ocean areas.

Most Selected Ships make and record in their meteorological logbook ocean current observations and observations of various meteorological, oceano-graphical and ornithological phenomena which they encounter. At the end of the voyage the logbook is collected from the ship by the Port Meteorological Officer and sent to his headquarters office, where all the meteorological data are extracted and used for climatological purposes, as was done when the Selected Ship Scheme started in 1853.

## Weather satellites

There are two main types of weather satellite – geostationary and polar-orbiting satellites. Geostationary satellites are placed in orbit above the equator at a height of approximately 36,000 kilometres, the period of their orbit results in the satellite remaining stationary over the same point on the

Earth's surface. Polar orbiters are in rather lower orbit and they circle the Earth at a height of approximately 850 kilometres.

The satellites provide images in both the visible and infra-red parts of the spectrum. The visible images are dependent upon sunlight reflected from the Earth's surface and are therefore not available at night. Visible images of higher latitudes in the 'winter' hemisphere are often very poor. The infra-red images are always available since they depend, not on sunlight, but upon the radiation emitted by the Earth and its atmosphere.

The satellites also carry equipment sensors to provide other information. This information includes measurement of sea state, water vapour images and temperature profiles.

Information from visible and infra-red images can be combined to provide information on cloud height and type, based upon the cloud texture and temperature. The images can also be used to assess the positions of fronts.

## Global warming

Observations of surface weather conditions also have an important role in research into the Earth's climate. Since the last quarter of the 20th century, there has been an increase in public concern about climatic change. It is well established that the quantity of carbon dioxide in the Earth's atmosphere has been steadily increasing, because this is a major end product when fossil fuels, such as coal, wood and oils, are burnt. Carbon dioxide is an important atmospheric gas because it is relatively transparent to short-wave radiation from the sun but absorbs long-wave radiation from the Earth and clouds. An increase in carbon dioxide should raise the mean temperature of the Earth because it prevents some of the outgoing radiation from leaving.

Identifying the effects of global warming is not simple since the Earth's climate is not constant. Over long periods of time, changes are known to occur due to the changing parameters of the Earth's orbit and the tilt of the Earth's axis. Major volcanic eruptions can put large quantities of volcanic dust into the atmosphere, the presence of this dust is associated with a cooling of the Earth's surface. Because of the difficulties in distinguishing the effects of global warming from the natural variability of the climate and predicting the likely consequences of global warming, the United Nations Intergovernmental Panel on Climatic Change (IPCC) was established in 1988 to advise world leaders on the seriousness of global climate change.

Computer models of the atmosphere are used in order to try to predict the effects of increased carbon dioxide. The results of these models vary but all agree that a global rise in mean temperature of about 1.5°C to 4.5°C is probable from a doubling of carbon dioxide. The differences are due to the way in which the models deal with factors such as clouds and atmospheric moisture. There are many possible feedback mechanisms. Melting of ice due to global warming would cause less solar radiation to be reflected and so would increase global warming. A rise in temperature would cause more evaporation from the ocean and since water vapour is a greenhouse gas this would increase warming. By contrast, an increase in cloudiness would increase the amount of incoming solar radiation reflected back to space and thus would reduce the warming.

Practically, the effect of such a rise in temperature would not result in a rise of mean temperature at every place on the Earth at all seasons, changes would be likely in the general pattern of weather systems and there would be regional and seasonal variations. Changes in the pattern of rainfall and the general weather would have important effects on agriculture and food production. The rise in sea level would have important implications for coastal communities.

The UK Meteorological Office has a website offering information at http://www.metoffice.gov.uk/. The World Meteorological Organisation has a useful site that has links to national weather organisations throughout the world. The address is http://www.wmo.ch/. Forecasts can also be found on sites belonging to newspapers and organisations such as the BBC: http://www.bbc.co.uk/.

## QUESTIONS

1 State what you know about the international scheme for the issue by radio of storm warnings, forecasts and general weather bulletins for shipping.

2 What is the value to the seafarer of giving details of existing weather in ocean areas in addition to a forecast for the same area?

3 Where do you find details about weather information for shipping broadcast by radio?

4 State what you know about radio facsimile apparatus, the meteorological information that it transmits and its value to the shipmaster.

# 19 FORECASTING THE MARINER'S OWN WEATHER

When direct and trustworthy forecasts for a ship's area of interest are being regularly received by radio from meteorological services ashore (and most ocean areas are covered today), the shipmaster should have no need to make his own forecast but it may well be useful for him to study a weather map to interpret the official forecast better. There may be occasions when he needs, for operational reasons, to make his own forecast (perhaps against the background of an official forecast) in order to decide what action, if any, he should take to avoid a weather hazard or maintain existing favourable conditions, in which it is essential for him to consult a synoptic map. Today, radio facsimile and the internet (see Chapter 18) make ready-made weather maps available to him.

Effective use of a weather map calls for a good understanding of the contents of Chapters 11 to 15 (inclusive), 17, 18, and this chapter, also for familiarity with the use of the Climatological Atlas, Admiralty Routeing Charts and Sailing Directions (Pilots).

## Frontal depressions

The energy to develop and sustain an active frontal depression is derived mainly from the air in the warm sector. Thus the deepening of a depression having a wide warm sector will usually continue to increase whilst unoccluded and often during the early stages of occlusion (See Chapter 13). Thereafter it can generally be expected to decrease as the occluding process continues. A fully occluded depression seldom deepens.

## Movement of depressions

See Chapter 13.

## Movement of fronts

The direction of movement is at right angles to the front.

## Speed of movement

A first approximation is obtained directly from the geostrophic wind scale by measuring the geostrophic wind component at right angles to the front.

The speed varies along the front and is maximum near the depression's centre, or wherever the isobars are closest together. Hence to plot the estimated future position of a front on a weather map, the geostrophic component should be obtained at several points along the front and adjusted according to the 'rules'.

In Figure 19.1 let the line $FF_1$ represent a front, AB and CD two consecutive isobars intersecting the front at points B and D respectively.

BE is perpendicular to the isobars and its length on the geostrophic wind scale is inversely proportional to the wind speed (W) shown on the scale.

Similarly the length of BD is inversely proportional to the required wind component (V) which is obtained by measuring BD on the geostrophic scale.

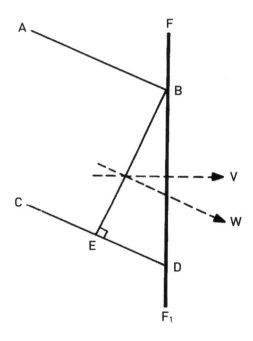

Fig 19.1

## Rules to assist in estimating the future position of a front

1 The speed of a cold front is usually about equal to, or a little more than, the geostrophic component. The more the pressure rises behind it the faster it moves.
2 The speed of a warm front is less than that of a cold front and is generally about two-thirds of the geostrophic value. The more the pressure falls ahead of it the faster it moves.
3 A front which is parallel to the isobars is slow moving or stationary.
4 When a front is stationary or nearly so, it tends to move from an area where the pressure is rising towards one where it is falling.
5 An occlusion advances roughly with the speed of the geostrophic wind component, but there is no definite rule.
6 An occlusion slows down when approaching a stationary (See **Blocking Conditions** in Glossary) anticyclone.

Provided successive weather maps are available the future position of a front can be easily estimated by **extrapolation** (that is, movement can be assumed to continue as shown by a succession of previous maps). It is recommended that this method should be used whenever possible; but consideration should be given to the foregoing rules and also to the likelihood of a change in the geostrophic wind during the forecast period. A close sequence of weather maps is very advantageous.

## Anticyclones

Formation and types of anticyclone are described in Chapter 15.

### Intensification and decline

1 The intensity of an anticyclone will not change:
   ❖ Whilst the pressure in the centre remains constant.
   ❖ If pressure on one side is rising at the same rate as it is falling on the other.
2 It is *intensifying* if:
   ❖ Pressure is rising all round the centre, or
   ❖ Pressure is rising on one side faster than it is falling on the other.

3 It is *weakening* if:
   ❖ Pressure is falling all round the centre, or
   ❖ Falling faster on one side than it is rising on the other.

## Movement of anticyclones

**1** Anticyclones are usually slow moving by comparison with depressions.

**2** An anticyclone or ridge between two depressions of a 'family' (see Chapter 13) travels with the same speed and direction as the depressions.

**3** An anticyclone formed in a surge of Pm (polar maritime) air behind the last depression of a family moves with the cold air mass, ie towards lower latitudes.

**4** A warm anticyclone moves slowly and tends to become stationary.

**5** Anticyclones move from areas of falling barometric tendencies towards areas of rising tendencies.

**6** The centre of an anticyclone tends to move towards the area in which the temperature is falling the fastest.

## Winds aloft

Some knowledge of the flow patterns in the upper levels of the atmosphere is useful in estimating the probable movement of depressions.

### Terminology

**Free atmosphere**
The atmosphere above the friction layer, ie above 600 metres above sea level, where the air motion is considered to be free from the effects of surface friction.

**Lower wind**
The wind at 600 metres, which level can be regarded as the base of the free atmosphere.

**Thermal wind**
The effect of horizontal temperature distribution on the upper wind, ie the vector difference between the upper and lower winds (see Figure 19.2). The thermal wind increases with increasing height, it flows parallel to the isotherms of mean temperature with higher temperature on the right in the northern hemisphere and on the left in the southern hemisphere. Its speed is proportional to the temperature gradient

**Upper wind**
The upper wind at any given level is a combination of the lower wind and the thermal wind at the given level.

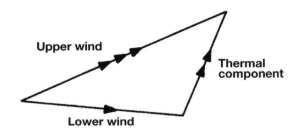

**Fig 19.2** *Vector diagram illustrating thermal wind.*

## Variation of wind with height

In the free atmosphere, the variation of wind with height is caused by changes in horizontal pressure distribution at successive levels; this in turn, for any given height, depends on the mean horizontal temperature distribution of the atmosphere below the given height. For a clearer understanding of this refer to Figure 19.3.

AB and CD represent two air columns of equal height and, for the sake of simplicity, standing on a surface of uniform pressure – say, 1,000 hPa.

The mean air temperature of column AB is warm, whilst that of CD is relatively cold, and therefore denser and heavier than AB. Thus the fall in pressure from B to A is less than from D to C, so pressure at A must be greater

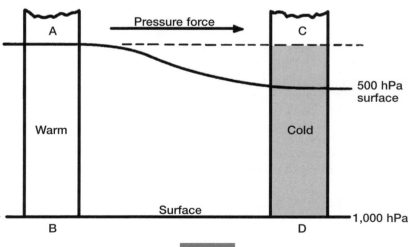

**Fig 19.3**

than at C. The pressure difference between the tops of two such columns of air increases, level for level, as height increases.

In areas where the temperature is high, the pressure at upper levels tends also to be high, and in areas of low temperature the upper air pressure also tends to be low.

The mean temperature of the troposphere increases from the poles towards the equator; hence the average thermal winds are westerly in both hemispheres (see paragraph on thermal wind) except within the tropics where conditions are more complicated. In very low latitudes the Earth's rotation is not effective and the geostrophic rule, on which the theory of thermal winds is based, does not apply. In addition there are other complications which go beyond the scope of this book.

The main distribution of winds within the tropics consists of a belt of easterly winds between the NE and SE trade winds; this belt extends over 10° to 20° of latitude and moves north and south with the sun. This easterly flow is modified in some regions by monsoon-like effects.

In general, in both hemispheres:

- ❖ Westerly winds normally increase with height.
- ❖ Upper winds tend to become increasingly westerly as height increases.
- ❖ Easterly winds normally decrease with height and later undergo a reversal of direction.

### Relationship between temperature and pressure at the surface

The relationship between temperature and pressure at the surface, as shown on a synoptic chart, can give a rough guide to the winds aloft by applying the following 'rules':

**1 When surface isotherms are parallel to the isobars:**

(a) *High temperature in region of high pressure.*

Wind increases with height with little or no change in direction.

(b) *High temperature in region of low pressure.*

Wind decreases with height and possibly undergoes a reversal in direction and then an increase with height.

**2 When lower wind blows across the isotherms:**

(a) *If lower wind blows from region of lower temperature.*

Upper winds back with height in the northern hemisphere (veer in southern hemisphere) and increase after a possible initial decrease.

(b) *If lower wind blows from region of higher temperature.*

Upper winds veer with height in the northern hemisphere (back in southern hemisphere) and increase after a possible initial decrease.

## Upper air charts

Today, with the ever increasing extent of the facsimile network (particularly in the southern hemisphere) and the growing number of ships being equipped with facsimile recorders and Internet access (see Chapter 18), the availability of upper air charts to the mariner is becoming more common.

There are several types of upper air charts and they are of particular value in the forecasting of developments at the surface. They indicate the large scale movements of air with greater accuracy and clarity than surface charts, which are complicated by small scale weather systems, topography and other local effects.

Constant pressure or contour charts show heights above mean sea level at which fixed (ie constant) pressures occur. Isopleths (see Glossary) of equal heights on a given pressure surface are called **contours** and they are usually drawn at height intervals of 60 metres, but at greater intervals on small scale charts covering very large areas.

Contour charts are most commonly drawn for the pressure surfaces of 1,000, 700, 500, 300, 200 and 100 hPa, of these the 500 mb chart is generally considered as being the most convenient for use by mariners. The clear indication of general windflow is useful in forecasting movement of pressure systems at the surface.

> Winds flow parallel to the contour lines, with greatest heights to starboard in the northern hemisphere and to port in the southern hemisphere.

Wind speed is directly proportional to the contour gradient (ie inversely proportional to the perpendicular distance between the contours) and reaches its maximum near the tropopause. *Note that 'highs' and 'lows' refer to heights, not pressure.*

### Long waves

A 500 hPa contour chart of the northern hemisphere will show a wavy circumpolar flow of westerly winds which tend to reach their greatest strength in the middle latitudes. The length of these 'long waves' (measured from crest to crest) varies considerably and some may exceed 3,700 kilometres. The amplitude of large scale troughs and ridges also show considerable variation during periods of a few days; if the north and south fluctuations become very large, closed circulations of air may form and become separated from the main stream. But there are sometimes periods of many days during which the position and shape of these long waves change very little. During such periods settled weather persists in areas south of the ridges (in the northern hemisphere); but within and a little to the east of the troughs the weather generally remains very unsettled throughout the period.

## Use of 500 mb (or hPa) contour chart for estimating movement of surface pressure systems

The contours indicate the general direction of movement of small scale surface pressure systems, such as warm sector depressions and cold ridges of high pressure between them. These systems travel at about half the speed of the winds at the 500 hPa pressure surface.

As depressions develop their closed circulations extend to higher levels, but the closed circulation of small shallow depressions are seldom evident on a 500 hPa chart.

The airflow round the long waves tends to guide surface depressions and anticyclones. If the airflow superimposed over either of these systems is straight in direction and steady in speed, they will be steered by this stream.

## Changes in upper air patterns

The movement of 'flat' upper air troughs and ridges (ie those having only slight curvature) is fairly rapid.

Upper air troughs and ridges of large amplitude with greatly curved contours move slowly.

The stronger and more extensive an upper air 'high' or 'low' the slower is its displacement.

In the northern hemisphere the circumpolar westerlies reach their greatest speed near the tropopause between latitudes 25° and 40°N during winter, and between 40° and 45° in summer. The average wind speeds are about 80 knots in winter and about 50 knots in summer when the thermal gradient is weaker. In the southern hemisphere the disposition of westerly winds is much the same as in the north.

In both hemispheres there are variations in speed due to local effects, eg in the vicinity of the south-east coasts of North America and Asia there is a very large temperature difference between ocean and continent; this increases the thermal component considerably and, in these areas, the westerly winds average about 100 knots in winter.

Figure 19.4 shows the contours of a 500 hPa pressure surface. It covers only a very small area on the original chart, from which some information has had to be omitted for the sake of clarity, and the scale has been considerably reduced to fit the book page. *Note the 'long waves' and closed contours mentioned previously.*

Figure 19.5 is a sample of the distance and geostrophic wind speed scales taken from the original contour chart. These scales have not been reduced.

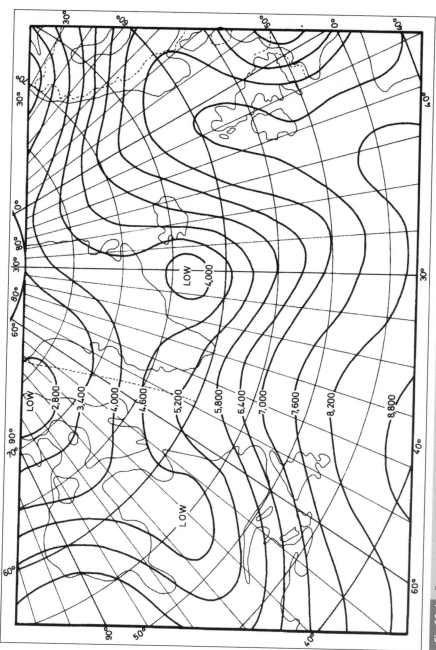

Fig 19.4 *Contours of 500 hPa pressure surface.*

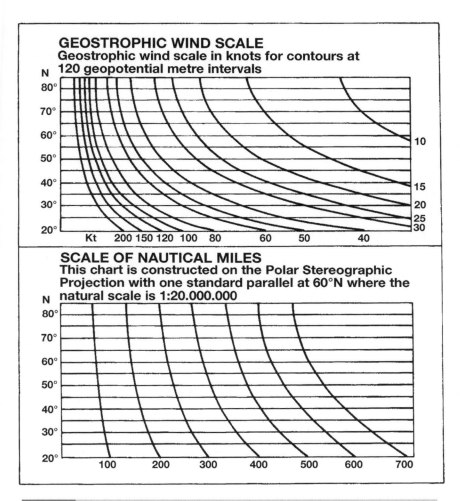

**Fig 19.5** *Geostrophic wind scale and distance scale (from Fig 19.4).*

*Our grateful thanks are due to the Meteorological Office, at Exeter, for their kind help and permission to use their chart for these illustrations.*

## QUESTIONS

1 Describe how you would measure the speed of movement of fronts drawn on a weather chart. What factors would you take into consideration when estimating their future positions?

2 Describe how a comparison of pressure tendencies in different parts of an anticyclone can give indication of an intensification or weakening of the system.

3 Discuss the movement of anticyclones:
(a) In general.
(b) Formed in cold Pm air behind the last depression in a 'family'.
(c) A warm anticyclone.
(d) An anticyclone or ridge between two depressions of a 'family'.

4 Of what practical value in forecasting is a knowledge of wind flow at upper levels?

5 Why are upper air charts of value in the forecasting of developments at the surface?

6 (a) Which pressure surfaces are commonly drawn by the meteorologist?
(b) In which direction does the wind flow in relation to the contours?

7 Discuss circumpolar long waves (Rossby waves) shown on a 500 hPa contour chart.

# 20 OCEAN SURFACE CURRENTS

The relationship between the surface currents of the ocean and the weather systems is so strong that no book on maritime meteorology would be complete without some description of surface currents. Much of our knowledge of ocean currents is derived from observations made voluntarily by officers in merchant vessels. The navigator needs some knowledge about these currents because of their effect on the safety and economical operation of a ship at sea. Ocean currents not only affect navigation but because some of them are warm and some cold they have an appreciable influence on climate and weather.

## Causes of ocean currents

The surface currents of the ocean can be divided into two main categories: drift currents caused directly by the wind and gradient currents caused indirectly by the wind or by density differences in adjacent areas. The wind is the primary agent which causes the currents; in general the more consistent the wind the steadier the current.

In the Indian Ocean and China Sea the surface currents are governed by the monsoons and therefore they vary seasonally in direction and strength. In the other oceans the main surface current circulation skirts the perimeter of the permanent mid-ocean anticyclone in the same sense as the wind; the prime mover of these currents in each case is the trade winds.

As a constant wind blows over the sea it tends to move the surface water along with it due to frictional drag. However the Coriolis force, which is due to the Earth's rotation, deflects this flow. Near the surface the water is deflected about 45° from the wind direction and this angle increases with depth. (See Figure 20.1.) Since the strength of the current decreases with depth the resultant effect in the whole depth of water affected by the wind is a deflection at 90° to the wind direction. The actual depth of water affected by the wind depends upon the strength of the wind and also upon the latitude. The deflection is to the right in the northern hemisphere and to the left in the southern hemisphere. Therefore a wind blowing from the north in the northern hemisphere produces a surface current which sets towards the south-west and the resultant deflection in the whole body of water is to the west. (See Figure 20.2.) It may appear that only the surface water effect is important for the navigator, however, it should be appreciated that the motion in the whole body of water is important for the general circulation.

A gradient current, as its name implies, is created by a pressure gradient or slope in the water level. This gradient may be due to a piling up of the water (eg against a coastline) or due to a density difference between two adjacent bodies of water. One of the most notable examples of a wind-induced gradient current is in the Gulf of Mexico where the west-going North Equatorial Current piles up the water near the coast and thus not only initiates the Gulf Stream but also enhances the Caribbean Countercurrent which flows eastward along the coasts of Panama and Colombia to Barranquilla.

Variations in the density of sea water may be due to temperature or salinity difference or a combination of both and when surface water of low density lies alongside water of a higher density a current will be created. In the western North Atlantic and Pacific the currents flowing out of the Arctic Ocean are basically density currents due to the relatively low salinity of the Arctic water, but assisted by a slight prevalence of northerly winds.

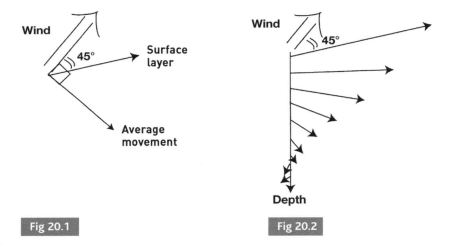

Fig 20.1

Fig 20.2

## Characteristics of ocean currents

In general, warm surface currents originate, as might be expected, in tropical waters while cold ones are born in the frigid zones. Probably the best known example of a warm current is the Gulf Stream, the extension of which, the North Atlantic Drift Current, brings warm water to Britain's shores and keeps northern Norway ice-free. A typical cold current example is the Labrador Current which extends down the east coast of the USA to Delaware Bay, inside the Gulf Stream and causing, off the Grand Banks of Newfoundland, a temperature gradient of up to 5.6°C (10°F).

In some places local cooling of the surface water is caused by a process called **upwelling**. When the surface waters tend to be drawn away from a coast by a persistent wind, cold water from below rises to replace it and this is known as upwelling and it results in a lowering of the surface water temperature. Upwelling is experienced off the coast of Chile and Peru, California, North-west Africa and South-west Africa. Upwelling brings nutrients to the surface and so all of these areas are rich in plankton. The plankton forms the basis of an extensive food chain.

Apart from seasonal changes, such as occur in the monsoon areas where the currents reverse in direction, there is much variety in the day to day direction and strength of almost all individual currents. Drift currents in particular are susceptible to wind variations and they are liable to temporary local increase or decrease in strength or even to reversal in direction at times. Even the Gulf Stream, which is the most constant current, may occasionally be affected locally in this way. The current roses depicted in the Ocean Current Atlases prepared in the Meteorological Office illustrate this variability. Some fax stations provide information on currents.

The maximum strength of currents, likely to be experienced in different parts of the main circulation in the open ocean varies quite a lot. In areas where the current is fairly variable, about 1 knot is the probable maximum and in areas where it is relatively consistent, rates of 2 to 3 knots may be encountered. In the Gulf Stream, Kuro Shio and Agulhas Current a 5 knot rate is sometimes present. The record is between 6 and 7 knots off Socotra, in the NW Indian Ocean, in August and September.

The rate of currents usually lies between about 2 per cent and 4 per cent of the wind strength, although the rate of the current depends to a large extent on the duration of the blow.

In coastal waters currents are often masked due to strong tidal streams.

## General surface current circulation

A picture of this is shown on the pull-out chart at the back of this book. The following is a brief summary:

### North Atlantic

The cool south-going currents on the east flank of the mid-ocean anticyclone merge into the wide band of west-bound current on the equatorial side and most of this turns northward on reaching the Caribbean to form the warm Gulf Stream, while a small portion turns east to help form the Caribbean Counter

Current. On the northern flank of the anticyclone the Gulf Stream fans out into the North Atlantic Drift Current, part of which eventually turns SE to complete the circulation while the remainder swings NE as far as the north coast of Norway. The flow of currents from and around the Arctic is a little complicated as can be seen from the chart.

### North Pacific

In most of this ocean the circulation is very similar to that of the North Atlantic; a cool south-going current on the east side of the anticyclone, a wide equatorial current flowing west on the south flank and the warm north-going Kuro Shio in the west, similar to the Gulf Stream, while there is an east-going current on the north side. On the extreme west of this ocean, however, in the area of the China Sea the currents flow NE or SW in accordance with the monsoons. As in the North Atlantic, there is a fairly diverse pattern of currents in the Arctic area.

### North Indian Ocean

The surface currents here are governed entirely by the monsoons, so that in the open ocean they flow eastwards during the summer (SW monsoon) and westwards during the winter (NE monsoon). In the extreme southern part of this ocean, close to the equator, the eastgoing Equatorial Counter Current flows eastward throughout the year. Close to the East African coastline there is a northerly current in summer and a southerly one in winter (the East African Coast Current, sometimes called the Somali Current); the summer current here may have a rate as high as 7 knots.

### Southern hemisphere

The surface currents of the South Atlantic, South Pacific and South Indian Ocean follow, in general, a regular pattern of anticlockwise circulation round the periphery of the permanent anticyclone in each ocean.

Each of these oceans has on its eastern side a relatively cold north-going current and a warmish south-going current on its western side; in each there is a fairly steady west-going Equatorial Current and Counter Current, but it is only in the South Indian Ocean that the Equatorial Counter Current is found south of the equator. The outstanding feature of the currents in this hemisphere is in the southern part of each ocean which combine to form what is called the 'Southern Ocean' where there is a very wide band of permanent east-going current encircling the world.

## Mediterranean currents

The general circulation of the surface water is counter-clockwise. It enters from the Atlantic, as a surface current, through the Strait of Gibraltar and flows thence along the North African coast. Due to the high rate of evaporation throughout the Mediterranean the salinity of the surface water gradually increases and it sinks.

Hence the outflow of this denser water through the Strait of Gibraltar to the Atlantic takes place below the surface inflow.

## Ocean currents

The list of currents in the following table should be studied in conjunction with the pull-out chart near the back of the book, which portrays the general pattern of ocean currents.

| | Atlantic Ocean currents | | |
|---|---|---|---|
| No | Name | Average Drift miles per day | Remarks |
| 1 | N Equatorial | 10–40 | Neutral temperature |
| 2 | Bahama | 10–50 | Neutral temperature |
| 3 | Caribbean Counter Current | 10 (average) | Neutral temperature |
| 4 | Gulf Stream | 10–70 | Warm at northern limit |
| 5 | N Atlantic Drift | 10–25 | Warm – considerable modifying effect on climate of Western Europe and the UK |
| 6 | Norwegian | | Warm |
| 7 | Irminger | 9 (average) | Neutral temperature |
| 8 | E Greenland W Greenland | 6–12 | Neutral – source of N Atlantic icebergs |
| 9 | Labrador | 5–20 | Cold – source of fog and icebergs on the Grand Banks |
| 10 | Canary | 10–35 | Cold – associated with upwelling |
| 11 | Azores | 11 (average) | Neutral temperature |
| 12 | Portuguese | 10 (average) | Cold to neutral |
| 13 | Counter Equatorial | 10–30 | Neutral temperature |
| 14 | S Equatorial | 10–45 | Neutral temperature |
| 15 | Guinea | 10–60 | Neutral temperature |
| 16 | Brazil | 10–35 | Warm |
| 17 | Falkland | 10–40 | Cold |

| No | Name | Average Drift miles per day | Remarks |
|----|------|------------------------------|---------|
| **Atlantic Ocean currents (continued)** | | | |
| 18 | Brazil Inshore Counter Current | 15 (average) | Cold – an extension of the Falkland current – may reach as far north as Rio de Janeiro in May to July |
| 19 | Southern Ocean | 0–30 | Neutral – carries S Atlantic icebergs – common to S Atlantic, S Pacific and S Indian Ocean |
| 20 | Benguela | 10–50 | Cold – associated with upwelling |

| No | Name | Average Drift miles per day | Remarks |
|----|------|------------------------------|---------|
| **Indian Ocean currents** | | | |
| 19 | Southern Ocean drift | | As on previous page |
| 21 | West Australian | 14 (average) | Inshore current sets south from March to August |
| 22 23 | Equatorial Counter Equatorial | 24 (average) | Do not reverse their directions with change of monsoon |
| 24 | Mozambique | 0–30 | Neutral temperature |
| 25 | East African coast | | Neutral. Average daily drift: November to January 16 miles February to March 48 miles May to September 48 miles *From July to September the daily drift may reach 170 miles (to the South of Socotra)* |
| 26 | Agulhas | 10–40 | Warm – a counter current is found close inshore |

**Note the change in direction with the change of the monsoon in the Red Sea, Arabian Sea, Bay of Bengal and the China Sea**. (See inset on chart for NE monsoon.)

| Pacific Ocean currents | | | |
|---|---|---|---|
| No | Name | Average Drift miles per day | Remarks |
| 27<br>28 | N Equatorial<br>Counter Equatorial } | 0–40 | Neutral temperature |
| 29 | S Equatorial | 24 (average) | |
| 30 | Kuro Shio | 10–50 | Warm – the 'Gulf Stream' of the Pacific |
| 31 | Oya Shio | 15–30 | Cold |
| 32 | Tsushima | | Warm |
| 33 | Liman | | Cold |
| 34 | Kamchatka | 5–10 | Cold |
| 35 | N Pacific Drift | 10–20 | Warm |
| 36 | Aleutian | 3–7 | Neutral temperature |
| 37 | Alaskan | 6 (average) | Neutral temperature |
| 38 | Californian | 10–30 | Upwelling occurs off the coast of California. Between November and December the Davidson Current sets northward close inshore |
| 39 | East Australian | Very variable 0–25 | Warm |
| 40 | Peru | 0–30 | Cold – upwelling along the coast |
| 41 | El Niño (Holy Child) | Variable | Warm – flows from January to March but is rather irregular |

NOTE: Detailed general and local information about ocean currents is given in the Admiralty Pilots and in the Ocean Current Atlases prepared in the Meteorological Office from information supplied by merchant ships. Monthly Admiralty Routeing Charts show clearly the predominant direction of sea surface currents for each quarter of the year, also the percentage constancy and the mean rate of current in knots in the predominant direction. Written information for the Atlantic is also available in Atlantic Pilot Atlas by James Clarke.

## QUESTIONS

1 Discuss the following:
(a) Wind-driven currents.
(b) Gradient current.
(c) Cold current.

2 Describe the effect of the Earth's rotation on ocean surface currents.

3 Name and describe the currents of the North and South Atlantic Ocean and give their average daily drifts.

4 Describe the general circulation of the surface currents in the Mediterranean Sea.

5 (a) Sketch two outline maps of the North Indian Ocean extending eastwards to include the China Sea.
(b) Illustrate the flow of ocean surface currents for the month of January on one map and for July on the other.

6 Describe how 'upwelling' is caused and name some notable localities where it occurs.

7 A drift bottle thrown into the sea on a voyage from Durban to Cape Town was eventually picked up on the north coast of Spain. Describe, in your opinion, the probable track it followed and name the currents which carried it until arrival at its final destination.

8 Name and describe the currents, including the average daily drifts, you would expect to encounter on a voyage from Christchurch, New Zealand to Rio de Janeiro, via Cape Horn.

# 21 SEA ICE

**Sea ice** is partly a meteorological and partly an oceanographic phenomenon. There are two kinds of floating ice encountered at sea: sea ice, formed from sea water; and icebergs, which break off the seaward end of glaciers and from shelf ice.

Sea ice is formed in all waters of the frigid zone in both hemispheres and in parts of the temperate zone in winter, particularly in the Antarctic. In springtime it breaks up and spreads into more temperate waters, notably in the Antarctic and western North Atlantic. Icebergs are, in general, born in the frigid zone in the North Atlantic area and in both the frigid and temperate zone in the Antarctic. In the Antarctic and western North Atlantic they drift well into the temperate zone during springtime.

## Physics of sea ice

The physics and development of sea ice are complicated. The freezing point of salt water is lower than that of fresh water and is governed by its salinity – the higher the salinity the lower the freezing point. Thus, in the open ocean, water with a salinity of 35‰ (parts per thousand) starts freezing at about −2°C (28.5°F), while in the Baltic, where salinity of 5‰ is common, the water starts to freeze at 0.3°C (32.5°F). Fresh water starts to freeze at 0°C (32°F).

The density of sea water increases with salinity. It also increases with cooling until a maximum density for the existing salinity is reached. The higher the salinity the lower the temperature of maximum density.

## Formation of sea ice

The cooling of surface water increases its density and it sinks, to be replaced by warmer, less dense water from below. The process continues until the whole column of water, from top to bottom, has attained its maximum density and all convectional descent ceases. Until this stage is reached ice cannot form. At sea it forms more readily where the water column is stratified into layers of different density. In this situation convectional sinking is confined to the topmost layer.

The maximum density of fresh water occurs at about 4°C (39°F). On the other hand, sea water with a salinity of 24.7 per cent, has its maximum density at its freezing point of about −1.5°C (29.5°F) and with higher salinity the temperature of maximum density decreases further. Therefore the formation of sea ice can be a lengthy process, especially in deep water with high salinity.

In some areas, despite very low temperatures, the winter is not long enough for the process to be completed and sea ice does not form. Sea ice first forms in shallow water where the delay due to convectional sinking is least.

## Development of sea ice

The development of sea ice begins with the formation of needle-shaped crystals called **frazil ice**. These crystals tend to float with their long axis vertical and they give the sea an oily appearance. The frazil ice crystals then thicken and congeal to form a greasy or soupy layer on the sea surface known as **grease ice**. Alternatively, falling snow crystals can produce **slush**. In the next stage, **shuga ice** develops, consisting of spongy lumps a few centimetres across. All the above are classified generally as **new ice**. This is followed by **pancake ice**, consisting of flat pieces, roughly circular in shape, often with a rim round the edge due to rubbing against adjacent pieces. The pancakes gradually join to form a more or less continuous ice sheet, called **young ice**; this can also be broken up by wave action.

Young ice eventually thickens and becomes **field ice** or **pack ice**, which is a generic term for all fully developed sea ice floating on the ocean and not attached to the shore; it varies in thickness from a few inches to several feet. Individual pieces of pack ice more than 20 metres across are called **floes** and the pack is termed 'open', 'very open', 'close' or 'very close' depending on the distance between the floes. Very close pack leaves little or no water visible. Pack ice originating in Arctic or Antarctic waters may be several feet thick and very uneven due to **hummocking** (piling up) by the waves. Detailed ice terminology is given in the *Mariner's Handbook* and it is important to know something about these terms so as to interpret ice bulletins.

## Icebergs

Arctic bergs are derived from the seaward end of glaciers; as the glacier extends out over the water the force of buoyancy breaks off pieces of ice and icebergs are 'calved'. These bergs are generally irregular in shape and may contain rock and soil debris.

Antarctic bergs are sometimes calved from glaciers, but the majority have broken away from the enormous ice shelf which fringes the continent. It is thought that the pieces of ice shelf break off due to seismic activity. These bergs are flat topped with steep sides and are known as tabular bergs because of their shape. These bergs are often several miles in extent and are a lustrous 'plaster of Paris' white due to trapped air.

Icebergs have only about one eighth of their volume above the water and are thus a menace to shipping. The term *growler* is used for small bergs, less than one metre in height above the waterline. Larger bergs with one to five metres above the waterline are known as *bergy bits*, with the term icebergs used for larger pieces of ice.

## Distribution of sea ice and its seasons

Figure 21. 1 shows mean and extreme limits of sea ice in navigable waters of the northern and southern hemisphere at different times of the year. A brief description is given in the following paragraphs. Details are in the relevant Admiralty Pilots. The season and intensity of all forms of sea ice varies considerably from year to year, being influenced by wind and weather in the relevant winter and spring and by ocean current vagaries.

### Grand Banks of Newfoundland

Pack ice may be encountered any time between February and May and icebergs between April and August. The bergs which affect this area are calved from glaciers on the Greenland coast during the previous summer. Those from the east coast are taken by the East Greenland Current down the coast, round Cape Farewell and up the west coast by the West Greenland Current where they spend the winter trapped in the pack ice. The following spring they are swept, together with the bergs calved from West Greenland glaciers, to the Grand Banks area by the Baffin Land and Labrador Current. The ice in this region is particularly menacing to shipping because of the high incidence of fog there in spring and summer. When they get south of the Grand Banks they melt fairly rapidly in the warmer water.

### Gulf of St Lawrence and River

Generally navigable from end of April until the end of November. There is often plenty of field ice during the early stages and icebreaker help is needed sometimes. The only entry is through Cabot Strait until about mid-June when Belle Isle Strait also is open.

### Hudson Bay

Usually open to navigation, with icebreaker help at times, from mid-June until mid-October. There may be quite a lot of ice during the beginning and end of the season.

### Eastern Seaboard of North America

In winter, ice may be present in the harbours as far south as Chesapeake Bay.

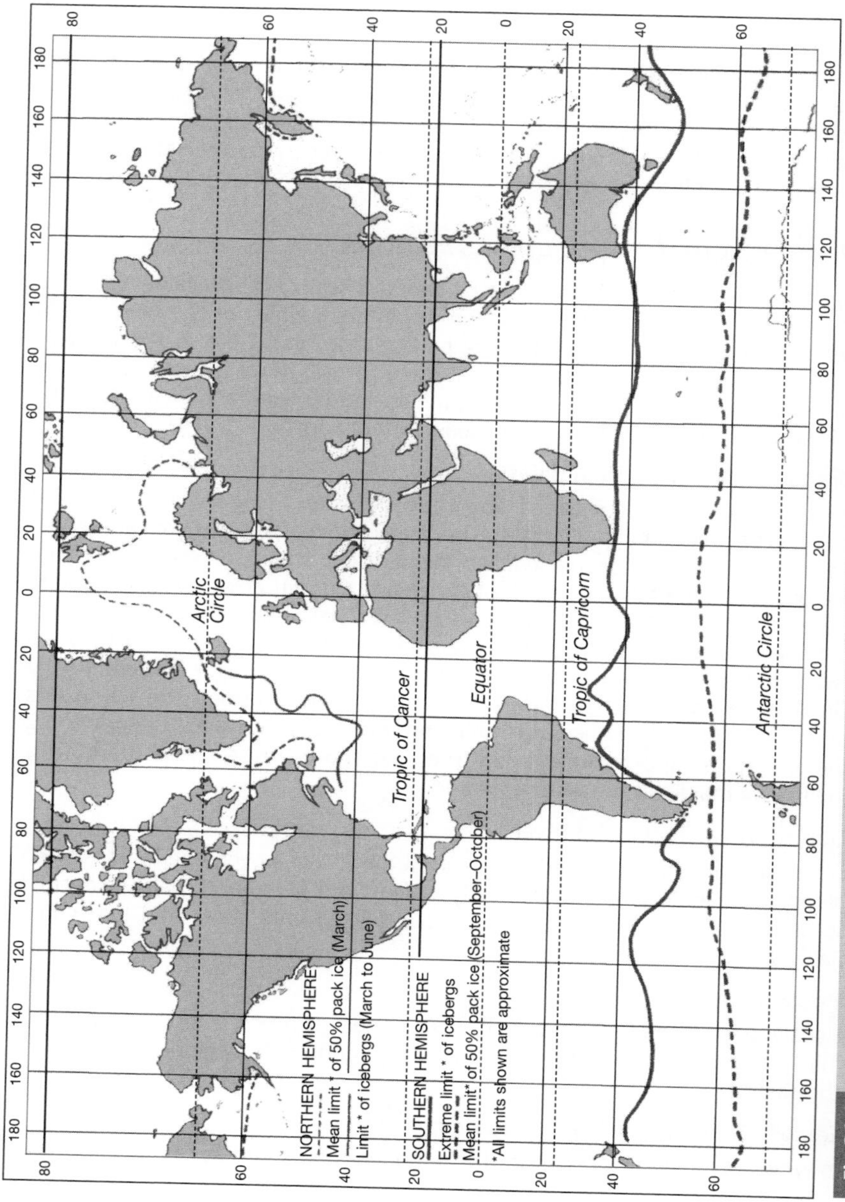
NORTHERN HEMISPHERE
Mean limit * of 50% pack ice (March)
Limit * of icebergs (March to June)
SOUTHERN HEMISPHERE
Extreme limit * of icebergs
Mean limit* of 50% pack ice (September–October)
*All limits shown are approximate
Arctic Circle
Tropic of Cancer
Equator
Tropic of Capricorn
Antarctic Circle

**Fig 21.1** *Limits of sea ice.*

### Denmark Strait

Pack ice may sometimes extend from Greenland to the Icelandic coast in winter and early spring.

### White Sea

Usually navigable from July to September; the North coast of Norway is usually ice-free, thanks to the effect of the North Atlantic Current.

### Baltic Sea

There is much ice normally in the northern and eastern portion from November to May; elsewhere only the coast itself and the ports are seriously affected, in midwinter and early spring.

### Black Sea

Liable to have some field ice in midwinter; in most years only the northern coasts are affected.

### North Pacific Ocean

In the area normally frequented by shipping, only the waters of the Japan Sea and northern part of the Yellow Sea are affected, and only by field ice, in winter months.

### Southern Ocean

The coasts of Antarctica are generally surrounded by a mixture of pack ice and icebergs throughout the year, impenetrable in winter and only navigable in midsummer by specially strengthened vessels. The probable mean limit of pack ice extends to about 55°S in places in mid-winter, but in mid-summer it recedes well south of 65°S except off Grahamland in the Weddell Sea area. The extreme limit extends north of 50°S in places throughout the year but never approaches Cape Horn or Cape of Good Hope.

The extreme limit of Antarctic icebergs reaches 35°S (between 30° and 40°W), while the mean limit is at a maximum of about 50°S in about 50°W. At all seasons bergs have been sighted between Cape Horn and Bahia Blanca. In the South Pacific bergs may be seen in about 50°S (between 120° and 180°W) and in the western Indian Ocean their mean limit in February and March is about 43°S.

## Ice warnings

Provided the ship is not in a specific cold sea surface current, sea surface temperatures might indicate the vicinity of pack ice. Thus a sea temperature of 1°C (34°F) might warn of an ice edge within about 150 miles; if the sea temperature were −0.5°C (31°F) the ice edge could be within 50 miles. Warning may be given by Ice Blink caused by reflection from the ice giving a glare in the sky near the horizon, mainly white if sky is cloudy, and yellow if sky is mostly blue; it is sometimes visible at night. In fog, white patches indicate ice at short distance. A noticeable reduction of sea and swell can warn of pack ice to windward. There may sometimes be a fog bank along the edge of pack ice. Small isolated chunks of floating ice may indicate field ice nearby. There is no similar indication of bergs. In all cases the only safe rule is to keep a very good visual lookout during the ice season. Bergs show up bright white on a clear dark night but there is always risk of growlers or bergy bits which will probably not be seen till very close, especially in high winds. Radar is not always reliable with an ice target – particularly with bergy bits and growlers when there is any sea clutter. On a foggy night if there is risk of meeting ice, the safest action is to stop the ship till the fog lifts or till daybreak. During the ice season in the western North Atlantic the International Ice Patrol, operated by the US Coast Guard, keeps watch on the bergs and field ice and warns shipping accordingly by radio broadcasts; aircraft are a major aid in this service. Radio warnings are also issued in Canadian, Baltic, Icelandic and Russian waters when necessary.

## Reporting of sea ice by shipping

The International Convention of Safety of Life at Sea prescribes that the master of every ship that sights dangerous ice must report it to other ships and to shore authorities as soon as possible.

## Icing on deck

The formation of ice on a vessel's superstructure causes a number of hazards. These hazards include a reduction in the vessel's freeboard and an increased likelihood of capsize if the vessel is heeled by the action of wind and waves. Antennae and lifesaving appliances are also adversely affected by icing.

Freshwater ice accretion is due either to the freezing of liquid rain or drizzle drops which come into contact with the vessel or snowflakes freezing onto the vessel. The weight of the ice added by these processes is relatively small and so the effects of freshwater ice accretion are not usually serious.

As the temperature is reduced below the freezing point of sea water there is an increasingly high risk of wind blown spray freezing onto the vessel. For this process to produce a significant hazard the sea temperature must be lower than 9°C and the wind speed must be at least Force 5.

Diagrams which can assist in estimating the rate at which ice accretion is likely to occur are printed in the *Mariner's Handbook*.

Further information about floating ice can be found at the websites of several organisations such as the British Antarctic Survey, http://www.antarctica.ac.uk/; the Canadian Ice Service, http://www.ice-glaces.ec.gc.ca/ and the International Ice Patrol, http://www.uscg.mil/lantarea/iip/home/html .

## QUESTIONS

1 (a) Describe briefly the development and general appearance of each of the following: frazil ice; grease ice; pancake ice; field ice (pack ice), floes.
(b) It is necessary to have some knowledge of ice terminology, so as to correctly interpret ice bulletins. Where do you find detailed ice terminology?

2 Compare the icebergs of the northern and southern hemispheres with particular reference to formation, calving, shape and size.

3 Describe the probable movement of an iceberg from the time of calving until final disintegration when formed on:
(a) the east coast of Greenland and
(b) the west coast of Greenland.

4 Which of the principal trade routes are affected by ice?

5 Where can you find details regarding sea ice conditions, seasons, etc, for any particular locality?

6 (a) Define roughly the extreme limits of icebergs for each of the following: N Atlantic, S Atlantic, N Pacific, S Pacific and S Indian Oceans.
(b) Define roughly the approximate mean limits of pack ice for each of the oceans mentioned in (a) above.

7 What action should be taken by the master of a ship on sighting dangerous ice?

8 What special precautions would you take when navigating in areas where you are likely to encounter ice?

9 Describe the various signs and phenomena which may give warning of the presence of
(a) Pack ice.
(b) Icebergs.

10 State what you know about the use of radar for detecting ice on ocean routes.

11 (a) What are 'bergy bits' and 'growlers'?
(b) When are they most dangerous?

# 22 WEATHER ROUTEING

The technique of weather routeing is that of using all available meteorological and oceanographic information to enable a vessel to make the safest, quickest and most economical passage. Climatological weather routeing implies taking advantage of favourable permanent and seasonal wind systems (eg trade winds and monsoons or prominent ocean currents), and this has been practised by shipmasters for hundreds of years. **The shortest route is not necessarily the quickest**. The modern form of weather routeing means taking advantage of the information derived by meteorologists from actual and forecast synoptic weather maps in order to avoid the worst of the weather in the mobile weather systems of the temperate zones. It seems not inappropriate, therefore, to refer to it as 'synoptic weather routeing'. This modern technique primarily involves trying to keep the ship clear of the areas of highest sea and swell waves, which are the main cause of speed reduction and of risk of damage to the ship and her cargo. A rudimentary form of this technique can be practised by a shipmaster himself nowadays by interpretation of the facsimile weather maps broadcast by radio from meteorological services. These maps portray actual and forecast wind force and wave heights along his route. Alternatively, the master can arrange to be given regular routeing advice by specialised meteorologists ashore, on a prepayment basis.

## Climatological weather routeing

The Indian Ocean, because of the reversal of direction and differing characteristics of the NE and SW monsoon winds with their resulting surface currents, has always been a fruitful area for climatological weather routeing.

First practised by the Arab dhows, then by sailing ships of western nations and then by power-driven ships, it is still used there fairly regularly today.

Other practical examples include the exploitation of the north-going Gulf Stream and south-going inshore current, respectively, off the United States east coast and of the route via the Azores for low-powered westbound Atlantic shipping.

Valuable advice about climatological routeing is given in the Admiralty publication *Ocean Passages for the World*. The International Loadline Zone Charts illustrate a compulsory form of climatological routeing in that they restrict the draught of ships in certain ocean areas during very unfavourable seasonal weather.

## Synoptic weather routeing

Formerly, information to enable mariners to plot their own synoptic charts was transmitted by radio in the form of a numerical analysis. However skilled were those plotting, this took a disproportionate amount of time on board. The result was also based on reports which would have been made several hours beforehand. This has been revolutionised by the access to facsimile weather maps which are now broadcast by radio by numerous national meteorological services. These can be received onboard by relatively inexpensive equipment and provide immediate up to date situations. In addition, it is possible for satellite transmissions to be received directly (see Chapter 19).

The master of a ship equipped to receive the facsimile maps has at his disposal, at 12-hourly intervals, maps prepared by experts showing actual and forecast wind direction and force with fronts, isobars and in the North Atlantic and Pacific, wave heights. Armed with these maps plus the written weather bulletins received by radio, he is better able than ever before to take evasive action. He is further helped in this by the relatively high speed of his modern ship.

## Weather routeing advice from meteorologists ashore

Synoptic weather routeing from the shore implies that, at the request of a shipowner, a meteorological service or commercial meteorologists advise the master of a ship, on sailing, as to the best initial route to take on the basis of the meteorological situation. They correct this advice if and when necessary as the voyage progresses. This technique was initiated in the USA and since 1954 the US Navy have regularly routed their military sea transport ships while US commercial meteorologists have provided a similar service to any merchant ships that pay for it. In 1960 a weather routeing organisation was started by the Netherlands authorities and in 1968 by the British Meteorological Office. These services have now expanded to comprise a range of forecasts as well as consultancy and advisory services. There are also private commercial operations offering similar services. The high degree of success attained by modern weather routeing from the shore has been made possible mainly by:

❖ The network of observations from merchant ships in the North Atlantic and North Pacific (especially the Atlantic).

❖ The availability of the high speed electronic computer to the meteorologist. This makes possible the rapid evaluation of present and future wind speed and wave contours, thus enabling him to look further ahead than ever before.

❖ The high percentage of merchant ships with speeds in excess of 15 knots. Relatively fast ship speed facilitates bold deviations on passage when necessary to avoid high wave areas.

❖ The availability of information regarding wave heights obtainable from satellite transmissions.

It is reasonable to suppose that a professional forecaster armed with so many facilities should be able to get more consistently good results than the shipmaster can on his own. The master of a fast ship in the North Atlantic cannot always spend time on weather maps and it may well pay him to restrict his own routeing to occasions when shore facilities are not available.

All authorities which provide weather routeing advice from the shore use broadly similar methods. The service provided needs to be tailor-made for the ship concerned. The first essential step is to prepare curves for each ship or class of ship that is to be routed, showing how much her speed is reduced in waves of various heights at the light and loaded draft. Specimen curves are shown in Figure 22.1. Such curves can be quite approximate and may, if not otherwise available, be constructed from data in the ship's logbook. In the case of a new ship, if curves were not prepared in the experimental tank, those from a similar class of ship might be used as a temporary measure. When a ship is being routed the meteorologist studies her performance curves against the background of the forecast wind and waves along the ship's intended route from a study of charts prepared with the aid of the electronic computer. He then prepares an initial '**least time track**' for as far ahead as he feels able to forecast, this may be anything between 24 and 72 hours depending upon the complexity of the synoptic situation. An example of a least time track is at Figure 22.2 showing some 48-hour least time track curves (plotted for 12 hour intervals) from Belle Isle towards Bishop Rock. In this case the advised track is the great circle because it cuts that part of the curve which is nearest to the destination. Obviously the most adverse conditions are to the north-eastward. This track may be modified in the light of other aspects such as surface currents, ice or estimated synoptic development during a further 24 or 48 hour period.

The master of the ship will be advised as to the recommended initial 'least time track' before sailing. This recommended route may be amended as and

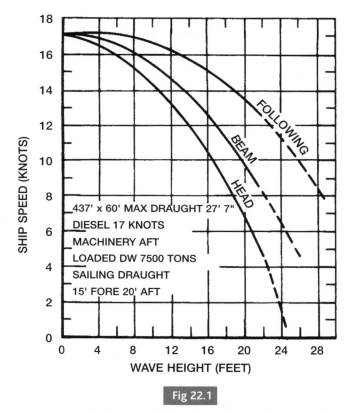

Fig 22.1

when necessary on the basis of further least time tracks prepared at 12 hourly intervals as the voyage progresses. It is essential that every ship that is weather-routed sends a weather message every six hours throughout the passage so that the routeing authority can follow her progress. An important feature of any such service is that the weather routeing team includes professional seafarers as advisors to the meteorologists.

The procedure in common use is as follows: the routeing service employs meteorologists who work in conjunction with master mariners with command experience in order to liaise with the master of each routed ship and to get details of the vessel's performance. This will include the vessel's speed, wave height curves, fuel consumption, probable draughts, the liability to carry deck cargo and any special requirements of the owners and master. The routeing service carries out the navigational work including calculating distances on alternative routes and the likely effects of adverse and favourable currents. They also keep up to date with ice conditions and ensure that routeing signals

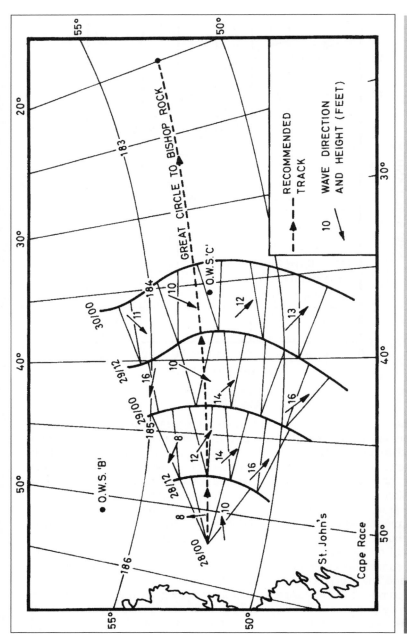

**Fig 22.2** *Some 48 hour least time track curves for a ship east bound from Belle Isle towards Bishop Rock.*

*Note: Intermediate meridians and parallels have been omitted here for clarity.*

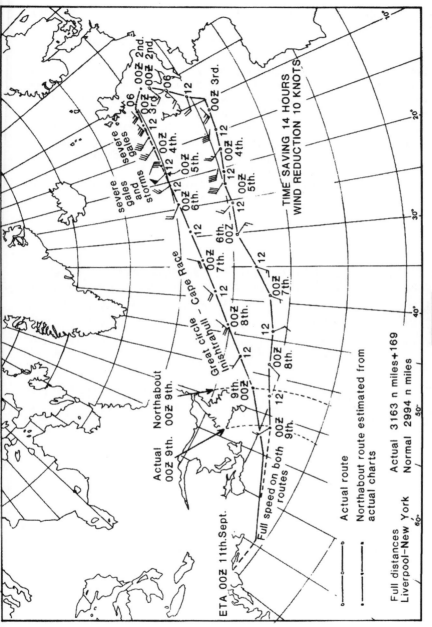

Fig 22.3

Note: 00Z indicates 0000 hrs GMT (UTC).

to the ship are unambiguous. Before the ship sails they give the master initial advice.

Communications play an important part in weather routeing and these are kept as brief and infrequent as possible so as to reduce cost. For example the initial signal to a ship sailing from Liverpool to New York might read 'Advise via FASTNET thence rhumb to 20°W thence circle Nantucket'. At the end of the voyage the master is sent a track chart showing the actual route and the winds experienced, also the winds that would have been experienced if the conventional route had been followed. (See Figure 22.3.) Experience has shown that despite adding as much as 300 miles to a 3,000 mile passage, both time and fuel can be saved. Just as important, there can be a considerable reduction in risk of damage to both ship and cargo.

A number of companies now provide weather routeing services, with an increasing number using the internet now that more ships have access onboard.

## QUESTIONS

1 What are the general principles involved in climatological weather routeing? Give examples.

2 Describe the modern methods of weather routeing and the information and facilities normally available to the shipmaster to enable him to practise his own routeing.

3 Explain, giving examples, why weather routeing is more beneficial on some voyages than others.

# 23 METEOROLOGICAL ASPECTS OF RADAR

Under certain standard meteorological conditions the range of merchant ship radars slightly exceeds the distance of the observer's visible horizon; using the same height of eye. However, just as the eye's range of vision is reduced by conditions of low visibility and may be increased by abnormal refraction, so also certain meteorological conditions affect radar range.

## Meteorological phenomena on radar

Since clouds consist of water droplets, rain falling from them will appear on a radar screen if it is sufficiently heavy. The larger the droplets the better the radar target it presents and the greater the interference it is likely to cause. Fortunately the droplets composing fog, mist and drizzle are very small and cause little interference. Showers will appear as light irregular shapes which are constantly changing, solid targets such as other vessels will be more persistent within these. Cold fronts in particular may show as a quite distinct formation. Heavy rain may temporarily cause a reduction in the potential range.

The composition of snowflakes is such that they do not cause as much trouble as heavy rain but this again is governed by flake size, intensity and extent of the snowfall. Solid particles such as sand and dust in the atmosphere may also diminish radar range. All these attenuation effects can, to some extent, be ameliorated by judicious use of gain control, though this action is liable to weaken the echo strength of any solid target such as a ship.

## Wave clutter

The presence of sea waves likely to cause clutter on the radar is obvious to those on the bridge. This indirect meteorological effect on radar performance is largely overcome by prudent manipulation of 'swept gain'. Nothing can prevent it, however, being a potential menace when the detection of small targets such as growlers, boats or buoys is concerned.

When heavy rain or some similar cause of interference is some distance from the ship, only objects inside or beyond the interference area will be liable to have their radar range diminished. The diffuse appearance of these attenuating echoes on the radar screen is easily recognisable and when remote from the ship their area has a hard edge. Very heavy rain often extends to considerable height; this enables the central dangerous area and eye of a tropical storm to be observed at extreme radar range (ie up to about 80 miles or so) and thus helps the mariner to take evasive action. (See Chapter 17.)

*Note*: Heavy rain can be penetrated by 10 cm radar but not by 3 cm radar.

## Standard atmosphere

Radar rays are affected by refraction when passing through atmospheric layers of varying density, to a greater extent than are light rays, which have a very much smaller wave length. The errors that can occur in astronomical navigation due to this bending of light rays at various altitudes are allowed for in navigation tables on the basis of 'mean refraction'. This assumes a uniform atmosphere with density decreasing regularly with height. Variations from this idealised state are ignored, except when a mirage shows abnormal refraction to be present resulting in accurate sights being more or less impracticable.

The effect of variations in refraction on a radar is to decrease or to increase its range. Normal radar performance, giving ranges slightly beyond the clear weather horizon at the radar's height of eye, can be expected in Standard Atmospheric Conditions (Standard Refractive Index). This implies normal convection and:

- ❖ A pressure at sea level of 1,013 hPa, decreasing with height at a rate of 12 hPa per 100 metres.
- ❖ A temperature at sea level of 15°C, decreasing with height at a rate of 0.7°C per 100 metres.
- ❖ A constant relative humidity of 60%.

These figures merely define Standard Refractive Index which implies a Standard Atmosphere and it is obvious that they cannot be checked by the mariner. They represent a mean value for the whole world and should not be considered as normal.

The refractive index, which indicates the degree of refraction in the atmosphere at any given time, depends on the density of the air through which the radar waves pass. Density, in turn, is governed by temperature, pressure and relative humidity. The greater the density the greater the refraction and vice versa.

## Standard propagation

In standard atmosphere the distance from the transmitter to the radar horizon is a little in excess of the optical distance. This distance is 2.21 $\sqrt{h}$ miles, where 'h' is the height of the radar scanner above the waterline in metres. Standard conditions exist mostly in temperate latitudes at sea well away from the land and when good mixing of the air is indicated by strong winds and cumulus clouds.

## Non-standard propagation

The effect of significant variations from standard conditions will either decrease or increase the effective radar range, according to whether the atmospheric density near the surface is less or greater than standard respectively. It is important for the mariner to know some of the meteorological conditions which are likely to affect radar propagation and what sort of unusual performance he might expect from his radar. Non-standard conditions are more commonly encountered in coastal areas near large land masses. A change in air temperature and/or relative humidity at any given height will cause a change in air density (and refractive index) at that height. If, however, we consider atmospheric changes which occur near the sea surface only, we can draw the following conclusions:

- ❖ An increase in temperature (which is the dominating factor) will cause a decrease in density and refractive index which will result in a reduction in radar range.
- ❖ A fall in temperature will cause the density to increase which will result in an increase in radar range.

## Sub-refraction

A cold air mass moving over a relatively warm sea rises in temperature at or near the surface. The result is a decrease in air density and a reduction in radar range. These circumstances imply a greater than normal decrease in temperature with height (a steep lapse rate), giving vigorous convection and an increase in relative humidity with height, evidenced by a convective type of cloud formation. In extreme cases the radar lobe may be refracted into an upward curve, away from the sea surface and can cause a reduction of 30 per cent or more in radar range. These conditions are most likely to be experienced in very high latitudes or near large very cold land masses in winter. Fortunately for the mariner, visibility tends to be good when sub-refraction is present, except when it is accompanied by heavy precipitation.

## Super-refraction

Warm, dry air moving over a relatively cold sea surface is cooled at or near the surface, thereby increasing the atmospheric density, which, in turn, causes an increase in refraction and radar range. When the sea is very cold relative to the air mass an inversion (see Glossary) may be formed. The resulting super-refraction may be further intensified if the warm air is very dry and picks up moisture from the sea surface. These conditions occur near large land masses in tropical latitudes and during spring and summer months in the temperate zone. In circumstances favourable for super-refraction there is a risk that if surface conditions are favourable, low visibility is liable to occur.

## Duct propagation

In extreme conditions of super-refraction the path of the radar ray may be refracted to such an extent that it assumes a downward curve which is greater than the curvature of the Earth's surface. On striking the sea surface the ray is reflected upwards and onwards, but is then refracted downwards to strike the water surface again and again in a succession of 'hops'. The energy is thus trapped in a 'radar duct' close to the surface and can follow the curvature of the Earth for very considerable distances, often causing echoes to occur on the second and third traces. Ranges of up to 100 miles can be attained sometimes on conventional targets. This phenomenon is somewhat similar to that which causes mirages.

None of these refraction anomalies has a very serious practical effect on radar performance from the navigator's viewpoint; they merely increase or decrease the extreme radar range, but it is useful to know when they are likely to exist and to be on one's guard against being taken by surprise when they occur.

### QUESTIONS

1  Describe the meteorological conditions which can cause:
   (a) Sub-refraction.
   (b) Super-refraction. What effect does each have on radar range?

2  What do you understand by 'standard propagation' in relation to radar range? Describe generally the regions and meteorological conditions in which it is most likely to exist.

3  Describe the effects of each of the following on radar echoes: fog, drizzle, snow and heavy rain. How can these effects be reduced?

# 24 METEOROLOGICAL FACTORS OF PLANNING AN OCEAN VOYAGE

## General principles

1 Choice of route must be balanced between considerations of safety and time, with emphasis on **safety**.

   The direct route is not always the shortest in time. A longer route with more favourable winds, currents and weather will often prove faster.

2 The regions, seasons, frequency and tracks of tropical revolving storms should be carefully noted.

3 Avoid areas where there are ice hazards or foul weather or a high percentage frequency of fog.

4 Avoid adverse currents and obtain as much advantage as possible from currents which are favourable.

5 Choose favourable prevailing or seasonal winds.

6 There is always the possibility of a long delay and/or damage resulting from bad weather. Thus it is prudent to plan for possible diversions for repairs, refuelling, etc.

## Recommended books

### Admiralty Sailing Directions (Pilots)*

Used for any coastal or 'small sea' passages (eg Caribbean, West Indies). These amplify in great detail the information given on the charts.

### Ocean Passages for the World*

As its name implies, this is specifically designed for mariners planning an ocean passage. It gives recommended routes and distances between the principal ports of the world. Details of winds, currents, weather, ice hazards, etc along each route are described. Much other useful information is included.

*Obtainable from Admiralty chart agents.

For coastal passages the navigator is referred to the appropriate Sailing Directions for the particular passage in question.

### The Mariner's Handbook*

This is an invaluable reference book containing chapters on the sea which include information on tidal movements and currents, one on general meteorology, including a reference to weather routeing, and two describing the full range of ice likely to be encountered by mariners, together with recommendations and duties when encountering ice.

## Monthly Admiralty Routeing Charts*

Monthly Admiralty Routeing Charts present the following information which is essential in route planning and on passage:

### Ocean currents

Predominant directions of flow for a stated period of the year are shown by arrows. Percentage constancy and mean rate (in knots) are also indicated.

### Winds

The following information is presented in each small area of the ocean, by means of a diagram called a wind rose.

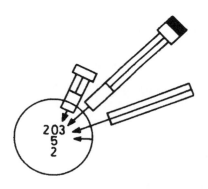

### Fig 24.1(a)

*It can be seen in this illustration that the wind blows most frequently from NE during the month for which the chart refers. The total length of the arrow against the scale shows a 40% frequency. (See Figure 24.1(b).)*

*Obtainable from Admiralty chart agents.*

(a) The direction from which the wind most frequently blows during the month is show by arrows which fly with the wind.

(b) Percentage frequency of each wind vector (direction and force) is indicated by the length of the arrow measured against a scale which is printed on the chart. (See Figure 24.1 (b).)

(c) The force of the wind (Beaufort scale) is indicated by the thickness and shading of the arrow shaft. (See Figure 24.1 (c).)

(d) The upper figure in the circle shows the number of observations. (See Figure 24.1(a).) The middle figure gives the percentage frequency of variable winds and the lower figure calms.

*Note*: For the purpose of clarity Figures 24.1 (a), (b) and (c) have been drawn to a larger scale than that on the routeing charts.

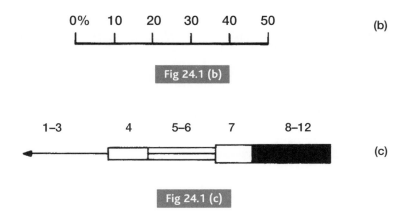

(b)

Fig 24.1 (b)

(c)

Fig 24.1 (c)

## Ice limits

(a) Minimum, average and maximum limits of pack ice.
(b) Mean maximum limit of icebergs.

## Shipping routes and distances

These are either between principal ports or at the ends of great circle tracks.

The following information is presented on small ocean charts inset over land areas on the main routeing charts.

## Fog

Isopleths show the percentage frequency of visibility of less than half a mile.

**Low visibility**

Isopleths show the percentage frequency of visibility which is less than 5 miles.

**Mean air pressure**

Mean pressure for the month is shown by isobars spaced at 2 millibar intervals.

**Mean air temperature (°F)**

Shown by isotherms printed at 10° intervals.

**Mean sea surface temperatures (°F)**

Shown by isotherms spaced at 10° intervals.

**Mean dew point temperatures (°F)**

Shown by isotherms printed at 4° intervals.

## QUESTIONS

1 List the meteorological factors you would take into consideration when planning a long ocean voyage, and name the sources you would consult for information.

# 25 BRIEF NOTES ON OBSERVATIONS AND INSTRUMENTS

## *The importance of being weather conscious*

Observing the weather is an essential part of the duties of a deck officer; for when on watch a part of the task of keeping a good lookout is to note and record changes in wind, sea, cloud, visibility, etc. In a sailing ship and in any small craft (such as fishing vessels), safety and progress depend almost entirely upon the wind and weather; the same is true but to a lesser degree aboard a power driven ship. It is no exaggeration to say that observing and recording the weather, and the intelligent use of simple meteorological instruments, is a part of seamanship.

The making of both instrumental and non-instrumental observations and recording them at least every four hours in the ship's logbook (and at the times of any significant changes) are a normal part of an officer's watchkeeping duties. It is particularly important to remember this as so many modern ships have totally enclosed bridges which can tend to isolate the mariner from the practical 'feel' of the weather.

### Non-instrumental observations

These include:

❖ Direction and force of wind.
❖ Direction and description of swell (the absence of swell should also be recorded).
❖ Visibility.
❖ Weather in general terms; eg fine, moderate rain, hail, etc.
❖ State of sky; eg blue sky, cloudy, overcast, etc.
❖ If the ship is taking spray or shipping 'green seas'.
❖ Behaviour of ship; eg rolling heavily, pitching, pounding, engines racing.

In merchant ships observations of wind direction and force, state of sea, swell and visibility are all *estimated*.

### Instrumental observations

Observations for the ship's logbook include:

* ❖ Barometric pressure reduced to sea level. The correction for diurnal variation is only applied to readings of barometric pressure for the master's operational use and so this correction should not be applied to the reading recorded in the ship's logbook.
* ❖ Air temperature
* ❖ Sea surface temperature. The method of obtaining the sea surface temperature should also be recorded.

### Observations by selected ships

If the vessel is a selected ship under the WMO voluntary observing scheme, more detailed observations are made and then coded for transmission. The message is coded using an international code, details of which appear in the Ship's Code and Decode Book Met. 0.509.

Selected ships' reports include barometric pressure, barometric tendency, air temperature, dew point (determined by table from hygrometer readings) and temperature of the sea surface, for all of which special instruments are supplied on loan to the ship by the Port Meteorological Officer. In a few selected ships distant reading instruments are supplied and fitted for all temperature readings, the recorders being sited on the bridge.

## Points to remember when reading a barometer

### Aneroid barometer

Tap gently, read, record and check. Correct only for Index Error and height.

### Precision aneroid barometer

Correct only for index error and height.

The correction table for height above sea level is entered with arguments height and temperature of the outside air, NOT the temperature inside the chart room.

## An approximate height corrrection for aneroid barometer

### Hectopascals

Height in feet above sea level increased by 10 per cent and divided by 30 gives the correction in hectopascals to be added.

Example:  Height of barometer = 30 feet
Therefore increase = 30 + 3 = 33 feet
Correction $\frac{33}{30}$ = 1.1 hPa

## Barograph

A barograph is supplied by the Meteorological Office to each Selected Ship. It produces a continuous graphical record of barometric pressure on a chart called a **barogram**. Thus it shows all fluctuations in pressure which occur between the fixed times at which the barometer is read.

It consists of a series of flat circular sealed metal boxes which are partially exhausted of air and are very sensitive to small changes in atmospheric pressure, which either increase or decrease the volume of the boxes. These movements are transmitted by an arrangement of levers to the vertical movement of a pen arm. The pen draws an ink trace on the barogram which is fitted round a revolving drum. The drum revolves about a vertical axis controlled by a clock, and one revolution takes one week, during which time a continuous record of all pressure variations are shown against GMT and date. The barogram is renewed every week when the clock is rewound.

The instrument is contained in a glass case with a hinged lid for winding the clock, renewing the graph, refilling the inkwell, etc.

The barometric tendencies read from the barogram are recorded in the meteorological logbook and included in the coded weather reports for synoptic hours. The barograph should be kept at Greenwich date and time throughout the voyage .

## Hygrometer

The hygrometer is an instrument for measuring the humidity of the air. The type most commonly used aboard ship (Mason's Hygrometer) consists of two ordinary thermometers mounted vertically inside a wooden box (Stevenson's Screen) which is louvred on all four sides to protect the inside from rain and sun, also to allow air to flow freely through the box.

The thermometers are exactly the same but one is 'dry' and is used for finding the air temperature, the other (the 'wet' bulb) has the bulb wrapped in a single thickness of muslin, secured round the neck of the bulb by a few strands of cotton wick, the lower ends of which are immersed in a small reservoir of distilled water placed in the screen; thus the wet bulb is kept moist by capillary action.

### How it works

The lower the humidity of the air (hence the drier the air) the faster the evaporation from the muslin on the wet bulb, hence the greater the difference between wet and dry bulb temperatures. Conversely, when humidity is high the rate of evaporation is slow and the difference in readings between the two thermometers, called 'the depression of the wet bulb', is very little.

The accuracy of the readings depends on the flow of air past the thermometers, so the screen should be exposed on the weather side of the bridge, well clear of warm air currents from deck, funnel, ventilators, skylights, etc.

The data derived from the readings of the dry and wet bulb thermometers are the **relative humidity** and **dew point** which are obtained from tables supplied with the instrument.

## Sea thermometers

The sea surface temperature is an important observation for the meteorologist as it is used for climatological work as well as for shorter term forecasting. A knowledge of the sea temperature is also useful to the shipmaster. It must be considered in controlling cargo ventilation and can assist in forecasting the onset of advection fog.

## Wind force and direction

Although some vessels are fitted with anemometers for measuring the wind speed these are difficult to site on a vessel as they should be kept clear of all obstructions. The motion of the vessel also affects their readings. The general method used is to observe the appearance of the sea surface. This is then compared with a detailed description of the probable state of the sea caused by winds of various forces as given in the Beaufort scale. This sea criterion was prepared by WMO. When using this method it is essential to take into account other factors which might influence the sea state. These include such things as fetch, tides and currents, depth and precipitation.

## Direction, period and height of sea and swell waves

These observations are difficult to make, but are important to the meteorologist. Like wind force and direction they are particularly difficult to make on dark nights and depend largely on experience. Despite the increased availability of wave height observations from satellites, observations from merchant vessels are still valuable.

## Cloud observations

The only way to become proficient in cloud identification is through careful study of the cloud descriptions and photographs, combined with much practice, for which every deck officer has plenty of opportunity when on watch. Detailed observations are needed from Selected Ships. (See Chapter 4.).

## Visibility

In Selected Ships visibility is recorded in kilometres/nautical miles on a scale of 0 to 9. When there is no target on the radar screen, this observation is largely a matter of judgement, having in mind the yardstick that the observer knows the distance from his ship to the horizon which can be mentally sub-divided. Although the horizon method is commonly used for distances of more than two miles, it is not always reliable because of the possibility of abnormal refraction.

On a long ship objects on board of known distances can be used when visibility is low. At night deteriorating visibility can be detected by a loom around the ship's navigation lights.

## Ocean current observations

These are asked for on a voluntary basis aboard Selected Ships of certain nations. The method is to calculate the difference between an estimated position with no current (ie DR position after making due allowance for leeway) and a reliable fix. The result is the set and drift of the current since the previous reliable fix.

# A METEOROLOGICAL GLOSSARY

**Abolute humidity**
(See also Humidity.) The water vapour content of air expressed in mass per unit volume, usually in grammes per cubic metre.

**Absolute temperature**
Temperature expressed in degrees according to the Absolute (Kelvin) temperature scale (freezing point 273 K, boiling point 373 K). Absolute temperature is obtained by adding 100 to any Celsius scale temperature.

**Adiabatic**
Without gain or loss of heat – thermally insulated. When a body of air is subjected to increased pressure it undergoes compressional heating; similarly, if the same body of air is subjected to a decrease in pressure it undergoes expansional cooling. In both cases, no interchange of heat takes place between the body of air and the surrounding air (environment); the temperature changes thus brought about are said to be adiabatic changes. If a parcel of air rises through its environment it undergoes a reduction in pressure and is cooled adiabatically. Conversely, if it sinks, it undergoes an increase in pressure and is warmed adiabatically.

**Advection**
The term generally refers to the horizontal movement of air, or the transference of heat by horizontal motion.

**Air mass**
An extensive body of air within which the temperature and humidity are more or less constant in a horizontal plane.

**Anabatic wind**
A local wind that blows up sloping ground that has been heated by the sun's rays. Favourable conditions are: a slack pressure gradient, strong surface heating, barren slope directly facing the sun. (See also Katabatic wind.)

### Analogue
A past synoptic chart which closely depicts the current situation for which the changes are to be forecast. Synoptic charts over a period of many years have been preserved and classified according to their particular patterns. Analogues are sometimes helpful as an aid to forecasting when there is a lack of other information. Meteorological history often repeats itself, and the developments which followed an analogue may sometimes be a guide to the possible developments in the future.

### Analysis
The process of positioning the fronts and drawing the isopleths (qv) on a surface or upper air chart.

### Anemometer
An instrument for measuring the speed of the wind.

### Anticyclone (also called a high)
An area of relatively high pressure surrounded by an area of relatively low pressure. Characterised on a synoptic chart by a system of closed isobars, roughly circular or oval in shape. The wind blows clockwise round an anticyclone in the northern hemisphere and counterclockwise in the southern hemisphere.

### Anticyclonic gloom
A condition of poor illumination by day resulting from a dense layer of stratiform cloud below the subsidence inversion of an anticyclone. It is most likely to occur during quiet winter weather in or near large industrial areas where there may be some smoke pollution.

### Anti-trades
The prevailing upper winds which blow above and in the opposite direction (polewards) to that of the trade winds.

### Anvil cloud
The anvil-shaped layer surmounting the top of a very well developed cumulonimbus cloud. Usually composed of ice crystals.

### Atmospheric pressure (See Pressure.)

### Backing
The changing of the wind in a counterclockwise direction (eg from W to SW). A clockwise change is termed a veer (eg from NE to E).

### Baguio
The local term for a tropical cyclone in the Philippine Islands.

## Bar
The unit of atmospheric pressure, being equal to a pressure of $1 \times 10^5$ pascals ($1 \times 10^5$ newtons per square metre).
1 bar = 100 centibars = 1,000 hPa (29.53 inches), formerly isobars.

## Baratic
The code word used in weather messages to indicate that the results of surface analysis follow in figure code. The term is now more widely used than this, however; a surface analysis chart broadcast by facsimile apparatus is often called a baratic. The word prebaratic refers to the surface forecast chart.

## Barometric tendency
The change in barometric pressure which has taken place during a specified period (usually three hours) before the time of observations.

## Beaufort scale
A practical means of estimating the force of the wind from the appearance of the sea. Ranges from a wind force of 0 'Calm' to Force 12 'Hurricane' and is used both by meteorologists when issuing forecasts and by seafarers when reporting on-the-spot conditions to shore stations.

## Bise
A cold dry wind which blows from the north-east, north or north-west in southern France during winter. The cold north-west wind, unlike the Mistral, is accompanied by heavy cloud.

## Black frost
A relatively dry air condition in which the ground temperature falls below freezing point but remains above the dew point of the air. Thus no deposit of hoar frost occurs.

## Black ice
The term usually refers to glazed frost which has formed on road surfaces. When drizzle or light rain falls onto a surface, the temperature of which is below 0°C, a thin sheet of clear ice forms.

## Blizzard
Falling or drifting snow driven by an intensely cold high wind.

## Blocking conditions
The normal westerly movement of weather systems in the temperate latitudes is sometimes 'blocked', for a few days at least, by a large stationary anticyclone whose circulation reaches to a high level. On the western zone of this system

the main flow of air is polewards and, on the eastern zone, equatorwards. This blocking situation gives persistent weather.

### Bora
A cold, often dry, north-easterly to easterly wind which blows down the slopes of the Dalmatian Mountains and off the eastern shores of the Adriatic. It is partly katabatic (qv), strongest and most frequent in winter, and sometimes attains gale force when the pressure distribution is favourable and the pressure gradient strong. Often dangerous when it arrives suddenly, with little warning, in the form of violent gusts.

### Buys Ballot's Law
If an observer stands with his back to the wind, the lower pressure is on his left in the northern hemisphere, and on his right in the southern hemisphere. Mariners usually say 'face the wind, and lower pressure is on your right in the northern hemisphere, and on your left in the southern hemisphere'.

### Chinook
A warm and dry south-west wind blowing down the eastern slopes of the Rocky Mountains in the USA and Canada. Its onset is usually sudden and the Föhn effect very pronounced, especially in winter when it causes rapid melting of the snow. (See Föhn.)

### Clear ice  (See Black ice.)

### Climate
The prevailing and characteristic meteorological conditions of a locality, as opposed to weather which is the state of the atmosphere at a given time. The climate of a locality is governed mainly by: (a) latitude; (b) position in relation to large land masses, oceans and temperature of ocean currents; (c) prevailing large scale wind circulations; (d) local topography; and (e) altitude.

### Cloud base
The level at which rising unsaturated air reaches its dew-point temperature. Further ascent above this level results in the condensation of excess water vapour, forming cloud. Height of cloud base is reported as height above ground level.

### Coalescence
Process by which small cloud droplets collide and combine to produce a large drop.

## Col
An atmospheric pressure distribution located between two highs and two lows arranged alternately. Associated with light variable winds; inclined to be thundery in summer and dull or foggy in winter.

## Cold anticyclone
One in which the air temperature at the surface and in the lower troposphere is, level for level, colder than in the air surrounding the whole system. In this type, the high pressure is caused mainly by the low temperature and consequent high density of the air. Probably the best example of a cold anticyclone is the winter high of Siberia. A transitory cold high may sometimes build up in the polar air in the rear of a family of depressions; usually they soon collapse but sometimes persist and, due to a long period of continued subsidence, slowly change into a warm anticyclone.

## Cold front
The line of discontinuity (at the surface or at upper level) along which an advancing cold air mass is overtaking and undercutting a warmer air mass.

## Cold sector
That area of a depression occupied by cold air at the surface. It comprises the whole depression after the occluding process has been completed.

## Cold wall
The sudden line of demarcation separating the Gulf Stream from the Labrador Current.

## Cold wave
A period of low temperatures (below the average for the season and locality) which lasts for 24 hours or longer, particularly during the cold season.

## Condensation level
The height at which rising unsaturated air becomes saturated. Further ascent causes condensation of excess water vapour forming cloud.

## Conduction
The transmission or flow of heat by direct contact.

## Confluence
The convergent flow and merging of adjacent airstreams.

## Convection
The transference of heat within a gas (or liquid) by movement of the gas containing it. In meteorology it is broadly understood as the vertical move-

ment of air within the environment, providing vertical exchange of heat and water vapour.

## Convergence
An area of convergence is one in which the horizontal inflow of air exceeds the horizontal outflow at the same level. In this condition the excess air escapes vertically, Except in arid regions, convergence at surface level is usually associated with much cloud and precipitation; typical examples are fronts and centres of depressions.

## Cordonazos
The local name for a tropical cyclone on the west coast of North America.

## Coriolis force  (See Geostrophic force.)

## Crachin
A weather condition which occurs between January and April in the China Sea and coastal areas from Shanghai to Cape Cambodia. The polar maritime air flowing down from the north interacts with trade wind and tropical maritime air, giving low stratus and drizzle with mist or fog.

## Cyclogenesis
The process whereby a new cyclone or depression is formed, or an existing one is strengthened.

## Cyclolysis
The disappearance or weakening of an existing cyclone or depression.

## Cyclone
A relatively very low pressure centre surrounded by an area of higher pressure. The wind circulates counterclockwise round the centre in northern latitudes and clockwise in southern latitudes. The term usually refers only to tropical cyclones which are limited to definite regions, in many of which they are given local names. Cyclones of the temperate latitudes are called 'depressions'.

## Cyclostrophic force
A centrifugal force which affects wind speed. It exists only when the isobars are curved and acts radially outwards at 90° to the isobars. Thus in a cyclonic circulation it acts against the pressure force and so makes the gradient wind speed a little less than the geostrophic speed. The reverse is true for anticyclonic circulation in which the cyclostrophic and pressure forces both act in the same direction.

## Depression (or low)

A central region of relatively low pressure surrounded by an area of higher pressure. The wind circulates anticlockwise round the centre of the low in the northern hemisphere, and clockwise in the southern hemisphere. The weather associated with a depression is, typically, unsettled with strong or gale force winds, much cloud and precipitation. The area covered by the system varies from about 100 to 2,000 miles in diameter. The term 'depression' usually refers only to depressions of middle or high latitudes, and 'cyclone' to tropical revolving storms. (See Cyclone.)

## Dew

A deposit of water formed by condensation on surfaces which have been cooled by radiation to a temperature below that of the dew point of the air. Favourable conditions are a calm night with a clear sky and high relative humidity.

## Dew point

The temperature to which unsaturated air must be cooled, at constant pressure and constant water vapour content, in order to become saturated. Any further cooling usually results in condensation of the excess water vapour. (See Frost point.)

## Diurnal variation

Changes which occur during a day, such as the variations in pressure and temperature.

## Divergence

An area of divergence is one from which the horizontal outflow of air exceeds the horizontal inflow at the same level; the deficiency of air is restored by vertical movement (subsidence, when divergence is at surface level). Usually associated with quiet settled conditions. The central area of an intense anticyclone is a good example.

## Doldrums

Oceanic regions between the NE and SE trade winds, and within which are light variable winds and calms accompanied by heavy rains, thunderstorms and squalls. They move north and south, following the sun, about 5° either side of their mean positions.

## Drizzle

Liquid precipitation in the form of very small water drops (between 0.2 and 0.5 mm in diameter) falling slowly and gently from low based stratus cloud in conditions of high relative humidity at the surface.

## Dust storms

Occur mainly in sandy deserts and semi-desert regions in the dry season, when there is an adequate supply of fine dust. The sudden arrival of a strong wind in very unstable air will carry dust to great heights and reduce visibility to less than 100 metres over a considerable area. Dust may be carried by the wind for great distances over the sea, causing 'dust fog' (or haze) to extend many miles from the coast.

## Elements (meteorological)

The physical forces of nature which together determine the weather: wind, rain, mist, etc.

## Etesians

This is the Greek name for the winds which blow, at times, from a direction between north-east and north-west in the Aegean Sea from May to October. The weather is usually fine and clear. These seasonal winds temper the summer heat. They are called the Meltemi by the Turks.

## Evaporation

In meteorology, the process of changing liquid water into water vapour.

## Eye

The central part of a hurricane.

## Fax

A method of transmitting and receiving charts by radio or telephone line. Abbreviation for facsimile.

## Fetch

The distance which the wind has travelled over a water surface in nearly the same direction.

## Fog

A condition of atmospheric obscurity caused by either water droplets, smoke particles, dust particles, or any combination thereof in suspension, in which the visibility is less than 1,000 metres.

## Föhn

A warm dry wind blowing down the leeward slopes of a mountain range. When moist air ascends the weather slopes to heights well above the condensation level, much of its original moisture may become trapped on the high ground, or deposited there by precipitation. Thus the air descending the lee slopes has a much lower moisture content; evaporation commences at a higher level than that at which condensation began. Below the 'evaporation level', warming takes place at the dry adiabatic lapse rate (1°C per 100 metres) and the air finishes its descent relatively warm and dry. The Föhn is a local name which originated in the Swiss Alps, but the effect is experienced anywhere where the conditions are suitable. A notable example is the 'Chinook' (qv).

### Free atmosphere
The atmosphere above the friction layer, ie above 600 metres above ground level, where the air motion is considered to be free from the effects of surface friction.

### Freezing fog
Supercooled (qv) water droplets of fog which freeze on impact with solid objects, forming rime.

### Freezing drizzle or freezing rain
Supercooled water drops of drizzle or rain which freeze on impact with solid objects to form glazed frost.

### Freezing level
The height above sea level of the 0°C isotherm.

### Friction layer
The layer of the atmosphere extending from ground level up to about 600 metres within which the effects of surface friction on air motion is appreciable.

### Front
The line separating warm and cold air masses. A surface front is the line along which the sloping frontal surface meets the Earth's surface. Although represented by a line on a synoptic chart it is, in fact, a narrow zone of transition.

### Frontal fog
Occurs at or near a front or occlusion. Caused by the evaporation of relatively warm rain drops falling through the cooler air below the frontal surface, thus increasing its moisture content and causing it to become saturated. See also Mixing fog.

### Frontogenesis
The development of a front or the marked intensification of an existing one. Convergence or confluence, or both (qv), are the most effective factors.

### Frontolysis
The disappearance or marked weakening of a front. Horizontal divergence is the most effective factor.

## Frost

Air frost occurs when the temperature of the air at screen level (about 1.2 metres above the ground) falls below 0°C. When only the air which is in contact with the ground falls below this temperature, the term ground frost is used.

## Frost point

The lowest temperature to which moist air at freezing temperatures can be cooled without deposition of ice from water vapour, when the pressure is kept constant. At the frost point the vapour is just saturated with respect to ice. With further cooling the vapour may be deposited on solid objects including other ice surfaces, as hoar frost. (See Dew point and Hoar frost.)

## Gale

A wind having a speed of between 34 and 40 knots – Force 8 on the Beaufort scale.

## Gale warning

Gale warnings are issued only when winds of Force 8 or above are expected. The terms severe gale, or gale becoming severe, indicate that winds of Force 9 or above are expected. The terms imminent, soon and later indicate within 6 hours, between 6 and 12 hours, and more than 12 hours, respectively.

## Geopotential

The potential energy per unit mass of a body relative to mean sea level. Geopotential height is used rather than a geometric height above sea level to allow for variations in the Earth's gravitational field.

## Geostrophic force

A deflecting force caused by the Earth's rotation. It acts on any moving body, always in a direction at 90° to its existing line of motion. It tends to deflect to the right in the northern hemisphere and to the left in the southern hemisphere. This force is not effective in latitudes within 5° of the equator.

## Geostrophic wind

A hypothetical wind in the free atmosphere which would flow parallel to straight equidistant isobars if they were stationary. It moves under the influence of two balanced forces – the horizontal pressure force and the geostrophic force (qv).

## Gradient wind

A hypothetical wind in the free atmosphere which would flow parallel to curved equidistant isobars if they were stationary. (See also Cyclostrophic force for its effects on the speed of the gradient wind.)

**Gregale**
A strong NE wind experienced in the central and western Mediterranean. It is capable of raising heavy seas which affect harbours having a northerly aspect in Malta and the east coast of Sicily, occurs mainly in winter when pressure is high to the north or north-west and low to the south. Usually lasts for 1 or 2 days and occasionally for 5 days.

**Ground frost**  (See Frost.)

**Gust**
A sudden increase in the strength of the wind. Its duration is very brief, being much shorter than that of a squall. At sea, gusts have no appreciable effect in raising waves, but squalls may last long enough to raise a group of waves which move along with the squall.

**Haar**
A wet sea fog which invades eastern Scotland and parts of eastern England, especially during summer.

**Hail**
Small balls or pellets of ice, usually formed in cumulonimbus clouds.

**Harmattan**
A dry and comparatively cool easterly wind which blows over north-west Africa during the dry season (November to March). It carries with it much dust from the Sahara, and reduces visibility for many miles to seaward. The period of the Harmattan decreases southwards.

**Haze**
Atmospheric obscurity caused by the presence of dust or smoke particles. The term is limited to conditions of visibility in which objects are visible at distances greater than one kilometre, but less than two kilometres.

**Hectopascal**
This is the appropriate SI unit for the expression of atmospheric pressure. Equivalent numerically to the millibar, abbreviated to hPa.

**Hoar frost**
A deposit of thin ice crystals or frozen dew upon surfaces whose temperatures have fallen below both dew point and 0°C.

## Horse latitudes
The regions of light variable winds, calms and fine weather of the subtropical anticyclones between latitudes about 30° to 40°. These belts fluctuate slightly north and south with the sun.

## Humidity
Absolute humidity is the water vapour content of the air expressed in mass per unit volume, usually in grammes per cubic metre. Relative humidity is the ratio of the existing absolute humidity to its saturation value at the same temperature, expressed as a percentage.

## Hurricane
The term applied to tropical revolving storms which occur in the regions of the West Indies, Gulf of Mexico, and off the north-east coast of Australia. Any wind of Force 12 (64 to 71 knots) on the Beaufort scale is termed hurricane.

## Hurricane wave (or storm wave)
The raising of the level of the sea surface, by something in the nature of 3–7 metres, in a confined region near the centre of a tropical revolving storm.

## Hygrometer
Instrument used to measure humidity or dew point.

## Hygroscopic nuclei
Very minute particles of chemical substances which tend to absorb moisture. They are always present in the atmosphere in varying amounts, and act as nuclei on which condensation of water vapour may take place forming cloud and fog. They consist mainly of salt from sea spray and other solid constituents in smoke from industrial and domestic fires.

## Icelandic low
A large area of mean low pressure centred between Greenland and Iceland. In January the mean surface pressure is about 994 hPa. Depressions frequently develop in this region but they are less intense during the summer months.

## Indraft angle
The angle between the surface wind and the isobars.

## Insolation
Energy received at the Earth's surface by short-wave solar radiation.

## Instability  (See Stability.)

## Intertropical convergence zone (ITCZ)

A narrow belt in low latitudes separating two convergent air masses which originate in different hemispheres. (Formerly known as the intertropical front, but as it bears little resemblance to fronts of the temperate latitudes, the term is now seldom used.) The zone fluctuates seasonally north and south with the sun, its range of movement being small over the oceans and large over the continents. Its mean position lies north of the equator for most of its length. Areas of horizontal convergence along this belt vary from day to day in both position and activity, but are generally associated with much cloud and convectional rain; for example, the doldrums of the Atlantic and Pacific Oceans.

## Intertropical front (See Intertropical Convergence Zone.)

## Inversion (of temperature)

An inversion, or negative lapse rate, is said to occur at a place when atmospheric temperature increases with increasing height through a layer. A surface inversion may be caused through radiation cooling of a land surface at night, or by horizontal movement of warm air over a relatively cool surface. An inversion at height may be caused by the subsidence and compressional warming of dry air from upper levels. In all cases, it indicates very stable conditions, upward movement of air being arrested at the level of the inversion.

## Isallobar

A line on a synoptic chart joining all points of equal barometric tendency. Isallobaric charts are used mainly to assist in forecasting the movements of pressure systems; for example, all depressions tend to move from areas of rising tendencies towards areas of falling tendencies (from isallobaric high towards isallobaric low).

## Isobar

A line of constant atmospheric pressure – expressed in hectopascals (hPa).

## Isogram (See Isopleth.)

## Isopleth or isogram

A line drawn on a map or chart and passing through all points at which the value of any particular element (such as temperature, dew point, barometric pressure, etc) is the same, eg isotherm, isobar.

## Isotherm

A line of constant temperature.

## Isothermal layer

A layer of the atmosphere in which the temperature lapse rate is zero.

## Jet stream

A very fast-moving current of air located near the tropopause (qv); usually in the nature of 1,000 miles in length, 100 to 300 miles in width, and having a depth of 3 or more miles. Speed at the centre of the 'tube' is often around 100 knots, and may sometimes reach 200 knots. Speed falls off very rapidly with departure from the central core of the stream. Jet streams are associated with a strong horizontal temperature gradient and they flow with both high temperature and high pressure (at upper level) on the right in the northern hemisphere, and on the left in the southern hemisphere.

In temperate latitudes, polar front jet streams flow in the warm air near to the frontal surface. They occur over a wide range of latitude but an individual jet stream usually persists for several days, sometimes more than a week, with little change of position.

Subtropical jet streams occur at a height of around 14,000 metres in latitudes 25°–30° in winter, and 40°–50° in summer. During a season they are fairly constant in position; they are very persistent in winter, and speeds exceeding 200 knots are not uncommon.

## Kata front

A front where the warm air is sinking down relative to the frontal surface.

## Katabatic wind

On a 'quiet' night with a slack pressure gradient and clear skies, a surface inversion resulting from radiation cooling may be formed. On sloping ground the air in contact with the surface becomes colder and denser than the air at the same horizontal level away from the ground. The denser air then gravitates down the slope forming a 'down-slope' wind. In this case, the cooling by contact overcomes adiabatic warming. The effect may be intensified considerably in winter months on mountain slopes where the descent over a snow clad surface is long; the resulting katabatic wind may then persist throughout the hours of daylight. Many local winds such as the Bora and Mistral, are greatly strengthened by katabatic drainage. (See also Anabatic Wind).

## Kaus

South-easterly winds which prevail in winter in the Persian Gulf. They are most frequent between December and April. Sometimes they are followed by a very strong south-westerly wind, called Suahili, which is dangerous to small craft.

## Khamsin

A hot dry, dust-laden southerly wind in the eastern Mediterranean blowing in front of depressions as they move eastwards along the Mediterranean or North Africa. They are most frequent from February to June. Gales in the Red Sea from south or south-west are also called Khamsin.

## Kharif
A strong south-westerly wind which, during the south-west monsoon, blows daily from about 2200 until the following noon in the Gulf of Aden. It frequently attains gale force during June, July and August.

## Land and sea breezes
The diurnal variation in sea surface temperature is usually very small when compared to that of the adjacent land. During the day, under the influence of solar radiation, the land becomes warmer than the sea. This inequality produces a pressure gradient near the coastline, and causes an onshore breeze (sea breeze) which is strongest during the mid or late afternoon. At night the process is reversed; terrestrial radiation cools the land to a temperature below that of the sea surface, the result is an offshore breeze (land breeze) which is usually weaker than the sea breeze, as the effect of surface friction is greater over the land.

Sea breezes may extend 15 miles on either side of the coastline; they rarely exceed Force 3 in temperate latitudes but may reach Force 5 in the tropics. Favourable conditions are clear skies and a slight pressure gradient. These winds, being local and transitory, do not conform to the general flow of surface isobars. If the general pressure gradient is strong the land and sea breezes may be completely masked.

## Lapse rate
The fall in atmospheric temperature per increase in height. The average lapse rate within the troposphere is about 0.6°C per 100 metres, but the actual lapse rate varies considerably from day to day and from place to place. Lapse rate is sometimes negative, ie temperature increases with height. This is called an inversion (qv).

Unsaturated air, when displaced vertically upwards through its environment, will cool at the dry adiabatic lapse rate of 1°C per 100 metres. Saturated air will cool at the saturated adiabatic lapse rate which varies according to temperature and pressure, but averages about half of the dry adiabatic lapse rate.

## Latent heat
The quantity of heat absorbed or emitted without change of temperature during a change of state of unit mass of a material.

Water may be changed to the vapour state by evaporation at any temperature but a supply of heat is required to effect the process. Since the temperature does not change whilst evaporation is taking place, the heat used is said to become latent and is stored in the vapour. The same quantity of latent heat is required irrespective of the temperature at which the change takes place. When evaporation takes place into the atmosphere heat is drawn from the surroundings or from the evaporating surface and can be transported from one level to another, or from one region to another. Much of the heat supplied to sea and land surface by solar radiation is used in the process of evaporation and contained in the atmosphere as latent heat; later cooling by ascent or by transportation into cooler latitudes may cause condensation and release of latent heat, thus raising the temperature of the upper air, or effecting transfer of heat from tropical to temperate latitudes.

### Leste
A hot, dry, southerly wind occurring between Madeira and Gibraltar and along the north African coast in front of an advancing depression.

### Levanter
An easterly wind in the Straits of Gibraltar, bringing excessive moisture, local cloud, heavy dews, poor or bad visibility, and sometimes rain. It can occur at any time of the year, but is most frequent in March and from July to October. The Levanter is generally associated with high pressure over western Europe and low pressure to the south-west of Gibraltar or to the south over Morocco. It is usually light or moderate in force, and a banner cloud extends for a mile or so to leeward of the Rock. On occasions, when it blows fresh or strong, dangerous eddies are formed in the lee of the Rock.

### Leveche
A hot, dry, sand-and-dust-laden southerly wind which blows on the south-east coast of Spain. It occurs in front of an advancing depression and its approach is often heralded by a belt of brownish cloud moving up from the south. (See also Scirocco.)

### Libeccio
The predominating westerly or south-westerly wind in north Corsica. It often causes high seas and may be accompanied by violent squalls. It is most persistent during summer months. In winter it alternates with winds from the north or north-east. (See Tramontana.)

### Line squall
A very well marked, particularly active cold front in the form of a V-shaped trough. Its approach and passage are characterised by an arc or line of low black cloud (often 'roll' cloud) preceding the front. A sudden freshening and slight backing of the wind, followed by a veer of perhaps 90° or more as it passes, together with a hard squall or squalls, often heavy rain or hail with thunder and lightning; it is also marked by a sudden fall in temperature. The barometer commences to rise rapidly immediately the trough has passed, the wind moderates quickly and tends to back a little before settling to a steady direction. A line squall generally lasts for about 15 minutes and occasionally for half an hour. (See Pampero and Southerly buster.)

## Long wave (Rossby waves)
A smooth wave-like pattern on an upper air contour chart, which shows the flow of westerly winds right round the Arctic low. These long waves vary considerably in amplitude and length, and may extend for 2,000 miles or more from crest to crest. There are generally four or five of such waves to be seen on a contour chart of a complete hemisphere.

The position and shape of long waves are of special importance in forecasting.

## Long-wave radiation (terrestrial radiation)
The ground is cooled at night by outward (long-wave) radiation in excess of incoming radiation. Conditions favourable for nocturnal cooling are: a cloudless sky, low absolute humidity, and absence of wind. Dew and hoar frost (qv) are indications of effective long-wave radiation.

## Loom
The glow of a light which is below the horizon, caused by reflection, such as from low cloud.

## Looming
1  An apparent elevation of distant terrestrial objects by abnormal refraction; objects below the horizon may become visible. Associated with a strong inversion. (See Mirage.)
2  Term used when land or objects are seen indistinctly through poor visibility, darkness or distance.

## Maestro
A fresh north-westerly wind which blows in the Adriatic in summer. It is accompanied by fine weather.

## Marin
A strong south-easterly wind in the Gulf of Lions. It is associated with depressions moving north-east or east from northern Spain or southern France. Usually it brings warm cloudy weather with rain.

## Meltemi  (See Etesians.)

## Mirage
An optical phenomenon in which objects appear to be raised, lowered, magnified, distorted, inverted or multiplied due to unusual and sharp variations in density of atmospheric layers close to the Earth's surface.

## Mirage, inferior
Occurs when the surface air is strongly heated by contact with hot, fairly level ground, and so becomes less dense than the air immediately above. Rays of light from the clear sky are refracted upwards towards the observer; the illusion produced is that of an expanse of shimmering bright water.

## Mirage, superior
When the surface is much colder than the air above, and the wind is very light, a strong temperature inversion is formed. In this case, the light rays from an object are bent downwards towards the observer, and objects below the horizon may become visible. Sometimes an inverted image is seen above the real object and occasionally, an upright image over the inverted one. Superior image occurs more often in high latitudes. (Beware of the effects of abnormal or subnormal refraction when finding distance off a 'rising' or 'dipping' light.)

## Mist
A condition of atmospheric obscurity caused by the presence of suspended minute water droplets. The term is limited to conditions in which objects are visible at distances greater than 1 kilometre, but less than 2 kilometres (1,100–2,200 yards).

## Mistral
A cold dry, strong N or NW wind blowing over the north-west coasts of the Mediterranean. It occurs usually when there is high pressure to the north-west, over France, and low to the south-east. It often attains gale force, especially in winter, when the flow of air over the Gulf of Lions is reinforced by katabatic drainage from the French Maritime Alps and also from the funnelling of the Rhone Valley.

## Mixing fog
Forms along the boundary (mixing zone) between two air masses of widely differing temperatures, both of which are nearly saturated. Sometimes called frontal fog because it is often experienced during the passage of a front.

## Mizzle  (See Scotch mist.)

## Monsoon
A seasonal wind blowing from a large land mass towards the ocean in winter, and in the reverse direction in the summer. Caused by the unequal surface heating of large land and sea areas. In the summer, low surface pressure develops over the relatively hot land; in winter, high pressure builds up over the relatively cold land. Monsoons occur in many parts of the world but those of the Indian Ocean and China Sea are the best known.

## Norther

A strong, cool, dry northerly wind which blows over the Gulf of Mexico, Central America and the western Caribbean. It is most frequent in the colder months of the year, and is associated with intense anticyclones over western North America and a depression over the Caribbean. Northers sometimes attain gale force.

## Numerical forecast

A forecast produced using a computer model of the atmosphere.

## Occlusion

Within a frontal depression the cold front moves faster than the warm front and eventually overtakes it. Thus, advancing polar air overtakes retreating polar air, and the tropical air of the warm sector is lifted off the ground. When these two polar air masses come together, their differing characteristics (due to recent history) will cause the overtaking air to override or undercut the retreating air; in both cases, the process is called an occlusion (warm or cold).

## Okta

Unit used in reporting cloud amount; it is equal to an area of one eighth of the area of the sky.

## Orographic cloud

Orographic cloud is formed when an airstream, on meeting a barrier of high ground, is deflected upwards and the consequent adiabatic cooling brings the temperature below the dew point of the rising air.

## Ozone layer

The layer of the atmosphere where the concentration of atmospheric ozone is greatest. The maximum concentration occurs between 20–25 kilometres above the Earth's surface.

## Pampero

The name given to a severe line squall in the Argentine and Uruguay. (See Line squall.) Most frequent between June and September.

## Polar front

The line of separation between the principal polar and tropical air masses in the temperate latitudes. Most of the travelling depressions of these latitudes are formed on bends or waves on the polar front. It often extends as an unbroken line for thousands of miles.

## Prebaratic

Term used for a forecast chart showing positions of surface isobars and fronts.

## Precipitation
The term includes rain, drizzle, sleet, snow, hail, dew, hoar frost, rime and glazed frost. Cloud, fog and mist are not classed as precipitation. 'Wet fog' however, which deposits water on the surfaces with which it comes in contact, is classified as precipitation.

## Pressure
Force per unit area exerted on a surface by the liquid or gas in contact with it. Atmospheric pressure at any level is produced by the weight of the air which lies above that level; hence atmospheric pressure decreases as height increases.

## Pressure gradient (horizontal)
The change in pressure per unit distance measured at right angles to the isobars. It is generally termed steep when the isobars are close together, and slight, slack or flat when they are widely spaced. The steeper the pressure gradient, the greater the wind speed. In the middle latitudes, a gradient of 1 hPa in 30 miles gives a geostrophic wind speed of approximately 30 knots (surface wind speed at sea about 24 knots).

## Pressure tendency
The rate of change of pressure with time. In practice it usually refers to the change in pressure during the period of three hours prior to the time of observation. Of great practical value in forecasting. (See Isallobar.)

## Prognostic chart
Forecast chart.

## Prontour
A forecast chart (upper air) showing the contours of an isobaric surface, eg 500 hPa prontour.

## Quasi-stationary front
A front whose position shows little or no movement on successive synoptic charts. Subject to wave-like disturbances which bring increased frontal activity and the likelihood of the formation of a new depression.

## Radiation (solar)
The transfer of heat from one body to another by electromagnetic waves. The heat of the sun is radiated through empty space to the Earth, this is short-wave radiation. The Earth radiates its heat into space in the form of long-wave radiation. By day the incoming radiation from the sun exceeds the outgoing radiation and the Earth's surface becomes warmer. At night there is no incoming radiation and the surface undergoes cooling throughout the period of darkness.

### Radiation inversion (surface inversion)
A layer in which temperature increases with height, extending upwards from the ground. A temperature inversion extending upwards from the ground and resulting from a period of nocturnal radiation cooling. Favourable conditions are: a clear sky at night, and little or no wind. The inversion will be greatly strengthened if the period of darkness is long, as in winter months.

### Radiosonde
A small, compact radio transmitter, attached to a free balloon for the purpose of obtaining upper air observations: usually pressure, temperature and humidity. Wind velocities can also be obtained, either by tracking the balloon with a radiotheodolite, or by radar echoes from a radar target (reflector) carried by the balloon.

### Relative humidity
(See also Humidity.) The ratio of the existing absolute humidity to its saturation value at the same temperature, expressed as a percentage.

### Ridge
A ridge (or wedge) of high pressure is a tongue-like extension of an anticyclone or high pressure area. It is generally associated with fair weather, similar to that of an anticyclone. Ridges travelling eastwards between two temperate latitude depressions are usually fast-moving, and the fair periods which they often bring are brief. Ridges extending from continental highs in winter, or from sub-tropical highs, are slower in movement and sometimes remain in one area for several days.

### Rime
When supercooled water droplets of fog strike solid objects such as trees, telephone wires, ship's masts, rigging and superstructure at temperatures below 0°C they freeze on impact, forming a deposit of white ice crystals. The deposit is rough in appearance and grows out to windward of the object.

### Roaring Forties
The prevailing westerly winds of the southern hemisphere which blow over the oceans in the temperate latitudes, on the poleward side of the 40th parallel.

### Rossby wave  (See Long wave.)

### Satellites (meteorological)
Geostationary artificial satellites, operating at a height of 22,000 miles, regularly observe and transmit meteorological information to Earth. This information includes air temperatures, water vapour content, radiation data, cloud

disposition (which depicts the shape of depressions, fronts and other weather systems) and also, when the sky is clear, sea ice and sea temperature.

These satellites are especially useful in observing conditions over ocean areas and those land areas where observations are sparse. They are of vital use in giving advance warning of tropical cyclones. The information they provide is shared internationally.

## Saturation
Air is said to be saturated when its relative humidity is 100 per cent. It should be noted that, at sub-freezing temperatures, the saturation value of absolute humidity is higher over water than over ice – thus air which is only just saturated with respect to water is supersaturated with respect to ice.

## Scirocco
The local name for a southerly wind in the Mediterranean. Originating in the desert regions of North Africa, it crosses the African coast as a hot, dry wind and often carries much dust. Blowing over the relatively cool water surface, it picks up moisture and tends to become stable; thus it reaches the northern coasts as a warm, unpleasantly humid wind, often with fog or low stratus.

## Scotch mist
A combination of drizzle and thick mist; most common in the uplands of Scotland, from whence it derives its name. Also frequent in Devon and Cornwall, where it is known as 'mizzle'.

## Scud (stratus fractus)
Ragged-looking low clouds of bad weather, which appear to move rapidly below rain cloud (nimbostratus) in strong winds.

## Sea breeze (See Land and sea breezes.)

## Sea smoke (Arctic sea smoke, frost smoke, steam fog, warm water fog, or water smoke)
When cold air flows over a relatively very warm sea surface, intense evaporation takes place into the air at the surface, so that its vapour pressure becomes greater than the saturation vapour pressure of the air immediately above. As convection carries the warmed surface air upward into the colder air, the excess water vapour is condensed and gives the appearance of steam or smoke rising from the sea surface. Occurs mainly in high latitudes (eg with cold air blowing over gaps in the ice pack), off eastern coasts of cold continents in winter, over inland seas, lakes and waterways in autumn.

## Secondary cold front
A trough of low pressure in the polar air following the first cold front of a depression. It marks the advance of fresh polar air which, due to recent history, is colder than the polar air immediately behind the primary front.

## Secondary depression
A small low which forms within the area covered by the closed circulation of a larger (primary) depression. It generally moves round its parent low in a cyclonic direction, following the main flow of isobars and often develops sufficiently to completely absorb the primary depression. Secondaries often form on a frontal wave and sometimes at the tip of the warm sector of a partly occluded depression. Non-frontal secondaries may form within an unstable polar air mass.

## Shamal
A prevailing NW wind which blows over Iraq, the Persian Gulf, and Gulf of Oman. Most frequent in summer, when the monsoon low is established over NW India. Generally hot, very dry, and associated with cloudless skies. It carries quantities of dust and fine sand from the desert, causing bad visibility. In the early summer it may persist for several weeks at a time. Seldom exceeds Force 7, except in winter when it sometimes reaches Force 9, and may be accompanied by rain squalls, thunder, and lightning. The onset of a Shamal is not usually preceded by any marked barometric tendency.

## Showers
Rain, hail or snow falling from isolated convection clouds and usually of short duration. The term shower in weather reports distinguishes it from intermittent or continuous precipitation from layer cloud.

## Sleet
1  In British terminology: 'Snow and rain falling together or snow which melts as it falls.'
2  In United States Weather Bureau terminology: 'Frozen precipitation consisting of transparent, rounded, hard, raindrop-sized grains of ice that rebound as they strike a hard surface. Also called ice pellets.' In United States popular terminology: 'A smooth coating of ice deposited by freezing rain; glaze.'

## Smog
Fog which is thickened and darkened by smoke pollution. In large industrial areas, a normal white or grey water fog is often changed into brown smog by smoke from furnaces and domestic fires. With the introduction of legislation requiring the use of cleaner fuels this is now all too frequently caused by traffic exhaust gases.

## Solano
An easterly or south-easterly wind which brings rain to the Straits of Gibraltar and the south-east coast of Spain.

## Solar radiation  (See Radiation.)

## Sounding (meteorological)
Observations of atmospheric properties by means of such devices as satellites, balloons or rockets.

## Southerly buster
The local name for the sudden squally onset of cold air which marks the passage of a well-defined, active cold front on the south and south-east coast of Australia. The NW wind in advance of the trough is light, warm and oppressive. The arrival of the SW wind is usually marked by a line of cloud, and sometimes by thunder and lightning; it commences as a sudden violent squall, and often blows with gale force for several hours before moderating. There is a large and rapid fall in temperature as the front passes. Similar to the Pampero of South America.

## Specific heat capacity
The specific heat of a substance is the number of joules required to raise the temperature of 1 kg of that substance by 1°C. The specific heat of water is higher than that of any other common substance; hence the gain or loss of a given quantity of heat brings about a smaller change in temperature of the sea than of the land.

## Squall
A sudden, very marked increase in wind speed, which lasts for a few minutes and then suddenly dies down. It is of longer duration than a gust (qv).
   *When using the Beaufort scale for the estimation of wind speed, the following criteria should be used for the reporting of squalls: 'A sudden increase of wind speed by at least 3 stages of the Beaufort scale, the speed rising to Force 6 or more, and lasting for at least one minute.'*

## Stability (atmospheric)
Stable air offers resistance to vertical displacement. In unstable air vertical movement is stimulated. If, in a stable atmosphere, a parcel of air is displaced upwards or downwards it will tend to return to its original level immediately the displacing force is removed. In an unstable atmosphere the parcel will continue to move in the same direction after the initial displacing force has ceased to act. Lapse rate is the governing factor which determines whether the atmosphere is stable or unstable.

Unsaturated air is stable when its lapse rate is less than the dry adiabatic lapse rate (DALR), and unstable when its lapse rate exceeds the DALR.

Saturated air is stable when its lapse rate is less than the saturated adiabatic lapse rate (SALR), and unstable when its lapse rate exceeds the SALR. (See Lapse rate and Adiabatic.)

The air is conditionally unstable when the environmental lapse rate (ELR) lies between the DALR and SALR. The degree of stability or instability depends not only on the ELR but also on the height of the condensation level which is governed by the dew point of the surface air.

In general, atmospheric stability is favoured by small lapse rates, and atmospheric instability by large lapse rates. Layer type cloud is associated with stable atmosphere; cumuliform cloud of great vertical extent is associated with unstable atmosphere.

### Standing wave
An air wave which is stationary or nearly stationary in relation to the Earth's surface. Usually associated with the flow of air over high ground or other obstructions.

### Steam fog  (See Sea smoke.)

### Stratopause
The upper boundary of the stratosphere. it is located at an approximate height of 50 kilometres.

### Stratosphere
The region of the atmosphere contained between the tropopause (average height about 7 miles) and the stratopause (average height about 31 miles). Within this region temperature does not decrease with height, but remains practically constant in the lower levels, and increases with height in the upper levels. Temperature in the stratosphere is not governed by convection or transference of latent heat, but it is increased in the higher levels by absorption of solar radiation by ozone.

### Sublimation
A direct change from water vapour to ice or from ice to water vapour.

### Subsidence
The slow downward motion of air which is warmed adiabatically during descent. In an anticyclone, the deficiency of surface air due to divergence is restored by subsidence which brings about great stability and an anticyclone inversion. (See Adiabatic.)

## Sumatras

Violent thundery squalls which occur in the Malacca Strait, usually at night, during the SW monsoon period. They are initiated by katabatic winds; the sudden shift of wind from a southerly direction and an increase in force is accompanied by heavy cumulonimbus cloud, heavy rain and a marked fall in temperature.

## Supercooled water droplets

Water droplets in the liquid state at temperatures below 0°C.

## Supersaturation

When the absolute humidity of an air sample exceeds its saturation value at its existing temperature, the sample is said to be supersaturated and its relative humidity is greater than 100 per cent. Condensation nuclei are always present in the atmosphere, and so supersaturation can very rarely occur to any marked degree.

## Synoptic chart

A weather map drawn at a fixed time.

## Synoptic station

A place where weather observations are made at fixed times in order that a synoptic chart can be produced.

**Tendencies** (See Barometric tendency.)

**Terrestrial radiation** (See long-wave radiation.)

## Thermal depression (thermal low)

A surface depression, the formation of which is caused by unequal heating of adjacent areas. Strong surface heating over islands and peninsulas in summer, or inland seas and lakes in winter. Monsoon lows are large-scale thermal depressions.

## Thermal wind

The wind at upper levels can be resolved into two components – the lower (geostrophic) wind and the thermal wind. The latter is the effect of horizontal temperature distribution.

The thermal wind increases with increasing height and flows along the isotherms of mean temperature with higher temperature on the right in the northern hemisphere and on the left in the southern hemisphere. Its speed is proportional to the temperature gradient.

## Thickness

The vertical separation between pairs of standard pressure levels; eg 500 and 1,000 hPa. At any given point, the value of thickness is governed entirely by the mean temperature of the air column separating the two levels; thus, the thickness in a region where the layer is warm will be greater than in a region where the layer is cold and dense.

Thickness charts show isopleths (qv) of equal thickness (called 'thickness lines'). Areas of 'high' or 'low' thickness may be enclosed by thickness lines indicating areas of high or low mean temperature for the layer concerned.

## Tidal surge

An appreciable increase in the height of the tide, above the predicted level, at the corresponding time and place, caused mainly by strong and/or persistent winds, especially those with a long fetch. At HW spring tides it can cause severe flooding in low-lying sites.

## Tornado

An exceptionally violent whirl of air which moves over land, causing great devastation along a very narrow path. The diameters average only a few hundred feet, and the paths anything from 300 yards to 300 miles, but usually less than 15 miles. They form in hot, moist thundery conditions and are associated with very violent convection in cumulonimbus cloud. Often accompanied by deluges of rain, hail, thunder and lightning. Although experienced in many parts of the world, they occur most frequently in the USA, in the plains to the east of the Rockies.

Very severe damage is caused by:

(a) The very powerful updraft which can lift heavy objects into the air.
(b) Exceptionally low pressure in the centre of the funnel which causes buildings to explode when 'struck' by its arrival;
(c) Wind speed of such ferocity that small objects become missiles with high penetration, and heavier objects become huge battering rams. Wind speeds are believed sometimes to exceed 200 knots.

## Tramontana

A cold, dry, northerly or north-easterly wind on the west coast of Italy and off northern Corsica. It is associated with a depression over the Adriatic in winter but does not often reach gale force.

## Trigger action

The initial disturbance which brings about convection in unstable (or conditionally unstable) air, eg orographic uplift of air, uplift at a cold front or the heating of air by contact with a warm surface.

## Tropopause
The boundary between the troposphere and the stratosphere. Its height varies from about 5 miles at the poles to about 10 or 11 miles over the equator.

## Troposphere
The lower layers of the atmosphere bounded by the tropopause. Characterised by a positive lapse rate, convection currents, cloud and precipitation. It is the layer within which most weather is experienced.

## Tsunami
Sometimes mistakenly called tidal waves, these are waves caused by sub-sea earthquakes or other sudden changes in the sea floor. The displaced water produces waves that propagate away from the disturbance at great speed. These waves can be very destructive.

## Turbulence
Disturbed motion of the atmosphere.

## Typhoon
The local name for a tropical revolving storm in the China Sea.

## Vapour pressure
The atmosphere is made up of a mixture of gases. Each gas exerts a pressure proportional to its density. Atmospheric pressure is the sum total of the individual pressures of these gases. That part of atmospheric pressure which is due to water vapour only is called vapour pressure.

## Veering
A clockwise changing of the wind direction. The term backing is used to describe changing in an anticlockwise direction.

## Vendavales
Strong SW winds off the east coast of Spain, and in the Straits of Gibraltar. Associated with advancing depressions from late autumn to early spring. Often accompanied by violent squalls, heavy rain and thunderstorms.

## Vertex of a TRS path
The most westerly point on the path of the storm's centre.

## Virga
Precipitation falling below cloud which does not reach the Earth's surface.

## Vortex
A whirlpool or eddy which tends to draw bodies towards its centre; eg the centre of a tropical cyclone, tornado or waterspout.

## V-shaped trough
A sharply defined cold front, with isobars in the form of a 'V'. (See Line squall.)

## Warm anticyclone
One in which the air temperature, level for level, is warmer than in the air surrounding the whole system. It is the most stable, persistent, and slow-moving of all pressure systems. The sub-tropical highs are warm anticyclones.

A temporary cold anticyclone may sometimes change into a temporary warm one due to continued subsidence. This occurs when a temporary cold high remains stationary for a long period. A warm high gives quiet settled conditions, often dry, fine, sunny and warm.

## Waterspout
The localised result of exceptionally strong convective instability over the sea. It forms under a very heavy cumulonimbus cloud, from the base of which a funnel shaped cloud descends and reaches down towards the sea which is whirled into violent commotion, causing a cloud of spray to rise immediately below the funnel. Some waterspouts may develop no further than this but with others the end of the spout reaches down into the spray cloud and forms a writhing column between the sea and cloud. The upper part of the spout usually travels along at a different speed to the part near the surface, thus after a few minutes the column assumes a slant, becomes less active, and breaks at about one third of its height from the surface; it then disappears quickly. The life cycle of a waterspout usually lasts from 10 to 30 minutes. Diameters vary from 6 to 60 metres but are usually less than 30 metres. Speed of movement is very slow.

Waterspouts are the ocean counterpart of tornados and, although generally much less violent, they are a hazard to shipping and a serious danger to any small craft. Their occurrence is more frequent in the tropics than in temperate latitudes.

## Wave clouds
Clouds which form in the crests of standing waves. (See also Standing wave.)

## Wave depression
A depression which forms at the crest of a wave on a front.

## Weather
The term generally refers to meteorological conditions (such as cloud, precipitation, mist, fog, sunshine, etc) at a given time, as opposed to climate which is the prevailing meteorological condition of a place or region.

## Wedge
A wedge (or ridge) of high pressure is an outward extension from an anticyclone, usually between two lows. The associated weather is similar to that of an anticyclone, but is short-lived when the wedge moves along between two travelling depressions. A broad wedge extending from a large intense anticyclone may sometimes persist for many days.

## Wind chill factor
The air may feel significantly colder than its actual temperature when there is a strong wind. The wind chill factor is often expressed in terms of an equivalent effective temperature.

## Zonal flow
Motion parallel to the parallels of latitude.

# METEOROLOGY AND CARE OF CARGO

One of the main tasks of the shipmaster is to deliver his ship's cargo in good condition at its port of destination. Provided the cargo is shipped in good condition, suitably packed and properly stowed, secured and ventilated, its only real enemy in a well-found ship is a meteorologically induced one. Violent waves and adverse winds may delay the ship or so damage her that water gets into a hold, or her violent motion may cause cargo to shift. Significant variations in the temperature and humidity in the holds may cause sweat damage. Cargo carried on deck is obviously vulnerable.

In this chapter suggestions are made as to methods of dealing with these dangers. The vast bulk of what was formerly general cargo is now containerised and this has revolutionised the carriage of goods by sea but the advice given here applies in a general way to all types of cargo except liquids in bulk and other very specialised cargoes.

## Heavy weather

The size and strength of modern ships and the strength of hatch coverings and design of ventilators are such that only with exceptionally high waves is sea water likely to get into the holds. Some shifting of cargo may well be possible with heavy rolling and there is the risk of deck cargo or even containers being swept overboard. Chapter 25 gives advice as to how the master can, by some form of weather routeing, seek to avoid the worst of the wind and waves throughout an ocean passage or in a particular weather system. If he does get involved in violent weather he can only use his skill as a seaman to nurse his ship.

## Purpose of controlling ventilation

Cargo damage due to climatic conditions includes such effects as mould formation, germination of grain, corrosion of metals, staining of textiles, etc, and may arise from condensation due to various causes.

The purpose of ventilation is to cool the cargo (or perhaps to warm it) so that no large differences between the temperature of the cargo and that of the atmosphere arise; to prevent accumulation of moisture in the air of the holds and thus diminish or prevent condensation in the holds and to remove flammable or noxious gases. To ensure correct ventilation ships' officers need to understand the relatively simple physical principles involved. The action to be taken will depend on the nature of the cargo and the climatic conditions prevalent during the voyage; sometimes ventilation is good practice and sometimes it is not.

## Hygroscopic and non-hygroscopic cargoes

A non-hygroscopic cargo contains no moisture, eg unpacked machinery, tinplates, galvanised sheets and pipes, pottery, glass, gas cylinders, canned goods. It does not change weight during the voyage. Although it cannot give off moisture it offers surfaces on which moisture will readily form if its temperature is below the dew point of the air in the hold.

Hygroscopic cargoes contain natural moisture. They originate in agriculture, forestry and fisheries and include some packaging materials. For example, cocoa beans might contain 6 per cent moisture when shipped, seasoned lumber 20 per cent and wheat 12 per cent.

For any hygroscopic cargo there is a relative humidity value at which the surrounding air is in equilibrium and will therefore neither absorb moisture from, nor give moisture to, the cargo. Thus if the relative humidity of the air is below this value the cargo will give up moisture to the air; if it is above this value then the cargo will absorb moisture from the air. Hygroscopic material should, in general be 'dry' on shipment, which means that it should not produce a storage atmosphere damper than 70 per cent relative humidity. If the temperature remains constant, a cargo of hygroscopic material will keep its storage atmosphere steady at a relative humidity corresponding to its moisture content, ie at the equilibrium relative humidity. For example, at a temperature of 20° (68°F), wheat containing 14 per cent moisture would have a relative humidity of 70 per cent.

Because air can contain so little moisture and a hygroscopic cargo so much, the moisture in such a cargo readily replaces the moisture in the storage atmosphere which is withdrawn and replaced by drier air due to ventilation. The relative humidity of the storage atmosphere of a hygroscopic cargo will rise only moderately with temperature increase, but its dew point will rise more quickly because warm air can hold more moisture than cooler air.

When a hold contains more than one kind of hygroscopic goods, moisture can be transferred from one to the other; for instance dried fruit stowed near lumber. The lumber's moisture content of (say) 15 per cent has equilibrium with storage atmosphere of 75 per cent relative humidity; the dried fruit might have moisture content 14 per cent to 18 per cent, in equilibrium with 55 per cent relative humidity. The net effect is transfer of moisture from lumber to fruit; consequently the fruit exceeds its optimum natural moisture content and may deteriorate.

In a loaded hold, temperature differences between ship's structure and cargo develop as the ship changes latitude or crosses areas of steep temperature gradient; some cargoes do not warm or cool as fast as the ship does. Condensation affecting cargo in holds depends on changes in air and sea temperature and dew point. Such effects are most likely to be met in areas of rapid sea temperature change, eg off the east coast of USA and Canada, off San Francisco, off the Cape Verde Islands and off the west coast of S America. The air at sea is rarely saturated, the average relative humidity being between 70 per cent and 90 per cent.

Moisture that causes damage to cargo in a ship's hold falls roughly into two categories: 'cargo sweat' and 'ship's sweat'.

## Cargo sweat

This occurs when the ship proceeds from a cold area to a relatively warm one and the cargo provides the condensing surface, while the ship's steelwork remains relatively warm and dry. Typical examples are as follows:

1  If a ship is loaded in a temperate port with granulated sugar for carriage across warmer seas the ship's steelwork temperature soon follows the rising temperature of sea water and atmosphere, but the cargo temperature lags behind. Soon some part of the cargo is cooler than the dew point of the external air; if the hold is then ventilated the sugar may be wetted through condensation and later set hard; ventilation should not take place.

2  If canned goods are loaded in winter at (say) San Francisco for passage through the Panama Canal, the goods will not be much warmer at the Canal than when loaded, while the outside dew point will have risen to (say) 23°C (73°F). The hold should not be ventilated during this passage because moisture in the warm ventilating air would condense on the cans, causing rust. However, this is an example of the difference when such cargoes are carried in containers. Such containers will not normally have ventilation facilities in themselves.

## Ship's sweat

This occurs when the ship goes from a warm area to a relatively cold one, when the ship's steelwork inside the hold may provide the condensing surface. For example, if bags of cocoa were loaded in West Africa for passage to Britain, the ship's steelwork assumes the temperature of the sea water and air as these fall, but the cocoa tends to retain its high loading temperature. As cocoa is a hygroscopic cargo it has its own storage atmosphere, depending on its moisture content and temperature. If it can be cooled at the same rate as the sea water and outside air, the dew point of its storage atmosphere will follow that of the cold steelwork and there will be no sweating. But if it stays warmer than its surroundings, its storage atmosphere dew point will stay high; its warmth will cause an upward current to carry damp air to the underside of the relatively cold deckhead, where its moisture will condense. This phenomenon is called 'ship's sweat'; the moisture is derived from the cargo.

To prevent ship's sweat a hygroscopic cargo needs to be 'dry' when loaded, ventilated with outside air and stowed so as to allow the ventilating air to cool it (no matter what that air's dew point is, provided it is colder than the cargo), so that the cargo temperature may be reduced to that of the ventilating air.

A simple general procedure to avoid ship's sweat is to ventilate whenever the external air is drier than the air leaving each particular hold; in other words when the dew point of the external air is lower than that of the air in the hold. Obtaining the dew point of the external air is fairly easy by using a wet and dry thermometer in a screen, exposed on the weather side of the bridge, associated with dew point tables. The dew point of the hold air is more difficult to measure, but it can be done by using a whirling psychrometer in the air issuing from the hold; a luxurious alternative is to use distant reading instruments, fitted in the holds and read on the bridge. If no instrumental aids are available, an arbitrary decision has to be made, depending on the nature of the cargo and the climatic changes likely to be met. **Generally, if the cargo is shipped from a hot climate to a cold one it needs ventilating; if from a cold climate to a warm one, don't ventilate.**

Sweat damage in a ship's hold can be due also to local heating or cooling within the ship. Cargo stowed near engine or boiler room bulkheads may get heated and, if hygroscopic, give off moisture which will condense if it contacts cooler metal goods or ship's steelwork. Alternatively, the steel structure of a general cargo hold in the near vicinity of a refrigerated space may be cooled below the dew point of the hold air and cause sweating on the cold steelwork. Damage due to such causes can be checked by judicious use of dunnage.

The temperature of general cargo stowed in insulated spaces not under refrigeration is little affected by changes in sea and air temperature during a voyage, so that the cargo stowed therein tends to retain its loading temperature. On such occasions there is generally no need to ventilate unless the cargo was loaded in a temperate country for discharge in a port where the air is warm and humid, in which case some ventilation should he used to raise the cargo temperature adequately before arrival at destination.

## Spontaneous combustion

Some hygroscopic cargoes such as fishmeal, bales of raw cotton and other fibres are liable, under certain conditions, to ignite spontaneously; coal is also subject to this danger. The ultimate stage of actual combustion is preceded by an abnormal temperature rise in some parts of the stowage, undue dampness being the original cause of the trouble. Early detection of an undue rise of cargo temperature may enable remedial ventilation to be carried out, but this needs to be done with great care because of the effect of air on combustion. **It may be wiser to shut off all ventilation to the hold concerned.**

## Containers

Two types of condensation can affect container cargoes: cargo sweat and container sweat. For condensation to occur there must be a source of moisture and a temperature gradient. The source of the moisture may be the cargo itself, the package, the dunnage, the container walls or the air trapped within it at time of packing. A temperature gradient may develop between the outside atmosphere and the air inside the container.

### Example

A container packed with cartons of canned goods has been stored in a warm humid atmosphere for some weeks. Doors are shut and the container is parked in the open. The sun heats the roof in daytime and warms the air between roof and cargo; the air is thus able to hold more water vapour derived from the relatively damp cartons. The temperature of the cans is much slower in rising; so they remain cold and the moisture condenses on them. During night-time the container roof temperature falls and gets colder than the air inside the container and this air deposits moisture on the inside of the roof; if enough is deposited or if the container is shaken or jolted, this moisture drops on the cargo. Day and night temperature changes may look like the diagram in Figure A1.1. If the source of moisture within the container is eliminated or if no temperature gradient is allowed to develop, there can be no sweat. To reduce sweat risk inside the container, the cargo, skin of container, packaging and wood dunnage, etc, should be dry when the container is filled. The only sure (but costly) way to avoid sudden temperature changes is by using temperature control in an insulated container. Some containers have double 'skins' in which air is trapped between 'skins' and thereby forms an element of insulation. Some containers have dehumidifiers and some are refrigerated.

When the doors of a container are shut it becomes virtually airtight and watertight. Thus rain, snow and moisture-laden air cannot normally reach the contents of a properly secured container but external atmospheric conditions can still affect it in several ways. Cargo may be exposed to the atmosphere for some time before being loaded into the container and will acquire equilibrium with the atmosphere and its moisture content. Once the container is loaded and doors shut the only way outside weather can affect the cargo is through temperature changes. Thus the container behaves rather as if it were hermetically sealed and any condensation occurring on any one voyage is a product of the temperature and relative humidity inside the container and the temperature gradient to the atmosphere outside.

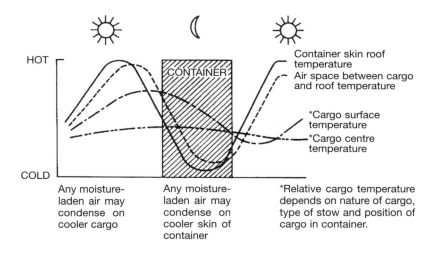

Container skin roof temperature

Air space between cargo and roof temperature

*Cargo surface temperature

*Cargo centre temperature

Any moisture-laden air may condense on cooler cargo

Any moisture-laden air may condense on cooler skin of container

*Relative cargo temperature depends on nature of cargo, type of stow and position of cargo in container.

Fig A1.1

# UNITS AND EQUIVALENT VALUES

## Inches – Hectopascals

| | |
|---|---|
| 29 in | = 982.1 hPa |
| N in | = (982.1 $N$ ÷ 29) hPa |
| N hPa | = (29N ÷ 982.1) in |

## Temperature conversations

C = degrees Celsius (Centigrade)
F = degrees Fahrenheit
A = degrees Absolute

$C = (F - 32) \times 5/9$     $F = (C \times 9/5) + 32$
$A = C + 273$              $C = A - 273$

## Some useful equivalents

### Distance

| | |
|---|---|
| 1 international nautical mile | = 6076.12 feet |
| | = 1852 metres |
| | = 1.852 kilometres |
| 1 kilometre | = 0.53996 nautical miles |
| 1 foot | = 0.3048 metres |
| 1 metre | = 3.2808 feet |
| 1 fathom | = 1.8288 metres |
| 1 metre | = 0.5468 fathoms |

### Speeds

| | |
|---|---|
| 1 metre per second | = 1.943 knots |
| 1 knot | = 0.515 metres per second |

## Liquids

| | |
|---|---|
| 1 litre | = 1,000 millilitres |
| | = 1.76 pints |
| 1 pint | = 0.568 litres |
| 1 gallon | = 4.544 litres |

## Pressure

| | |
|---|---|
| 1,000 hPa | = 29.53 in |
| 1 hPa | = 0.02953 in |
| 1 in | = 33.864 hPa |
| 1 lb/in$^2$ | = 70.3 gm/cm$^2$ |

## TABLE 1 — CORRECTION TO BE APPLIED TO THE OBSERVED BAROMETRIC PRESSURE FOR DIURNAL VARIATION WITHIN THE TROPICS

**LATITUDE ZONE 0° to 10° N or S**

| Local Time | 0000 | 0100 | 0200 | 0300 | 0400 | 0500 | 0600 | 0700 | 0800 |
|---|---|---|---|---|---|---|---|---|---|
| hPa | − 0.6 | − 0.1 | + 0.3 | + 0.7 | + 0.8 | + 0.6 | + 0.2 | − 0.4 | − 0.9 |
| in | − 0.018 | − 0.003 | + 0.009 | + 0.021 | + 0.024 | + 0.018 | + 0.006 | − 0.012 | − 0.027 |
| Local Time | 0900 | 1000 | 1100 | 1200 | 1300 | 1400 | 1500 | 1600 | 1700 |
| hPa | − 1.3 | − 1.4 | − 1.1 | − 0.6 | + 0.1 | + 0.7 | + 1.3 | + 1.5 | + 1.4 |
| in | − 0.038 | − 0.041 | − 0.032 | − 0.018 | + 0.003 | + 0.021 | + 0.038 | + 0.044 | + 0.041 |
| Local Time | 1800 | 1900 | 2000 | 2100 | 2200 | 2300 | 2400 | | |
| hPa | + 1.00 | + 0.5 | − 0.1 | − 0.6 | − 0.9 | − 0.9 | − 0.6 | | |
| in | + 0.030 | + 0.015 | − 0.003 | − 0.018 | − 0.027 | − 0.027 | − 0.018 | | |

**LATITUDE ZONE 10° to 20° N OR S**

| Local Time | 0000 | 0100 | 0200 | 0300 | 0400 | 0500 | 0600 | 0700 | 0800 |
|---|---|---|---|---|---|---|---|---|---|
| hPa | − 0.5 | − 0.1 | + 0.3 | + 0.7 | + 0.8 | + 0.6 | + 0.2 | − 0.3 | − 0.8 |
| in | − 0.015 | − 0.003 | + 0.009 | + 0.021 | + 0.024 | + 0.018 | + 0.006 | − 0.009 | − 0.024 |
| Local Time | 0900 | 1000 | 1100 | 1200 | 1300 | 1400 | 1500 | 1600 | 1700 |
| hPa | − 1.1 | − 1.2 | − 1.0 | − 0.5 | + 0.1 | + 0.7 | + 1.1 | + 1.3 | + 1.2 |
| in | − 0.032 | − 0.035 | − 0.030 | − 0.015 | + 0.003 | + 0.021 | + 0.032 | + 0.038 | + 0.035 |
| Local Time | 1800 | 1900 | 2000 | 2100 | 2200 | 2300 | 2400 | | |
| hPa | + 0.9 | + 0.3 | − 0.2 | − 0.6 | − 0.8 | − 0.8 | − 0.5 | | |
| in | + 0.027 | + 0.009 | − 0.006 | − 0.018 | − 0.024 | − 0.024 | − 0.015 | | |

CAUTION: When entering a barometric pressure in the log, or when including it in a radio weather report the correction for diurnal variation must not be applied.

# INDEX

# REEDS MARINE ENGINEERING SERIES

These books are obtainable from nautical booksellers, chandlers or direct from:

Macmillan Distribution Ltd
Brunel Road
Houndsmill
Basingstoke
RG21 6XS

Tel: 01256 302699
Fax: 01256 812521/812558
Email: mdl@macmillan.co.uk